FALCONRY
PRINCIPLES & PRACTICE

Roger Upton

A & C Black · London

TO JEAN AND S.W.F.

First published 1991 by
A & C Black (Publishers) Ltd
35 Bedford Row, London WC1R 4JH

© 1990 Roger Upton

ISBN 0 7136 3262 3

Acknowledgements
Thanks to M. L. Upton for his help
with the photographs.

A CIP catalogue record for this
book is available from the British Library.

Typeset in Fournier by
ABM Typographics Limited, Hull.
Printed and bound in Great Britain by
Butler & Tanner, Frome.

Contents

Contents

Foreword

As the reader will discover, much of what follows refers to flights with the larger of the long winged hawks: the peregrine, the saker, the lanner or the gyrfalcon. However, the chapters on training, furniture and housing are in general applicable to all species of hawk. The use of falconry terminology has been reduced to a minimum, and it is hoped that the indiscriminate use of the words 'falcon' and 'hawk' will not confuse the reader.

To enjoy the best of what falconry has to offer a whole-hearted commitment is required. There is no other sport that brings the practitioner so close to nature, and none that is so rewarding. Falconry is not for those who would dabble on the fringes of the sport; it is better left to the real enthusiast who practises the sport for no other reason than that he and his friends derive great pleasure from doing it well.

It is only by maintaining high standards that we can hope to ensure the survival of the art of falconry so that future generations can enjoy its principles and practice.

Roger Upton
Plough Cottage

NOTE Throughout the book falconers are referred to individually as 'he'. This should, of course, be taken to mean 'he or she' where appropriate.

Introduction

Falconry is the art of flying trained hawks at wild quarry in their natural environment. The objective is to fly a suitable hawk at selected quarry in the right type of country, so that a sporting flight results. Falconry is the finest of all the field sports, but only if it is practised in a skilled and sporting manner. It is a dramatic and spectacular sport, and because of this it attracts attention both from those who want to do it well and, unfortunately, from those who would make an exhibition of the sport and exploit it for commercial gain. The exhibitionist does little to further falconry as a sport, and only encourages a fringe interest. Falconry is not a sport that can be put away until the weekend, and any casual interest should be discouraged for the sake of the hawk that is involved.

Suitable country for game hawking

You will need suitable country to fly a hawk at quarry. For game hawking, provided that you can afford the ever-increasing rentals paid for sporting rights, there are grouse moors or partridge manors available, but it is important to make it quite clear from the start of negotiations that you intend to fly hawks over the ground. You will require several acres of suitable ground to fly hawks throughout the season, or indeed for five or six consecutive weeks. The minimum would be 3,000 acres or so, because although hawks do not disturb game as much as shooting does, falconers and their dogs, particularly if they are noisy, do disturb the ground. Also, it is better not to fly the same coveys day after day. Far too often a would-be falconer gets terribly excited

Peregrine in flight

about a piece of ground he has managed to obtain, and proudly shows you two or three coveys, fondly imagining that they will be sufficient for his needs; if his hawk is any good this certainly won't be enough.

In acquiring land, try to be a sportsman by making sure that you do not spoil another falconer's sport by hawking on adjoining ground, unless he is happy that you do so. It is even less sporting to 'poach' another man's ground. Always remember that there is a legal season for game, and that the 12 August or the 1 September is certainly early enough to enter a grouse or partridge hawk.

Suitable country for rook, seagull or magpie hawking is perhaps easier to find and is certainly cheaper to obtain permission for. It should never be forgotten that permission is needed to hawk over any land in Britain, and that to go poaching is to let down every other falconer. It is sometimes hard to accept a refusal to hawk rooks for example, especially when you know that the farmer or landowner regards them as little more than pests. However, it can be difficult to convince shooting interests that you will not touch their game birds and are only interested in hawking rooks or crows. Of course, accidents can happen and it is surprising how often a partridge will get up at just the wrong moment when shooting guests are out.

Hawking out of the hood

A very great area of suitable land is needed for hawking out of the hood. Rooks and crows in particular are very wary, and after they have been hunted a few times they will move off as soon as they suspect that a hawking party is approaching. The amount of land required for flying goshawks or broad winged hawks at rabbits, or for flying a sparrow-hawk or a merlin, is very much less, and no doubt suitable land can be obtained at little or no expense with polite enquiry. It is just as well to remember that permission given to hawk over land for free should not be taken for granted, and the least the falconer can do is to give the landowner an occasional gift at Christmas.

Obtaining permission to hawk over land

All too often it is easy for a flight to end on land where you do not have permission. Get off the land as soon as possible and, if the landowner or his keeper comes up to see what you are doing, explain the situation and apologise. More than one keeper has been relieved to discover that the telemetry receiver and aerial you have been waving about is not a television detector, and the result of a friendly discussion might well extend your hawking ground. One of the difficulties in asking for permission to hawk over land is that the owner, possibly his friends and probably his keeper if he has one, will all want to come and watch. They will understandably want to see, for example, whether you do indeed catch crows or rooks as you claim. It is doubly important that you at least show a good flight on such occasions, and that you do not turn up with an untried, unentered hawk.

Depending on casual invitation for your hawking ground invariably means that you often have a large and uneducated audience, which is far from ideal. A minimum 'home' base of suitable country for your choice of hawking is essential so that you can accept an invitation, confident that your hawk will at least do her best and so help to maintain the image of falconry as a positive and practical field sport.

Many years ago a friend of mine had a trained male golden eagle. His main quarry was rabbits (rather like using a sledge hammer to crack a nut!), but at that time myxomatosis had greatly reduced the chance of a flight. On enquiry at a small hill farm close to a mining village, my friend was given permission to fly at rabbits, but on seeing the eagle in the boot of the car the farmer enthusiastically asked if it would chase dogs, as he was continually being bothered by pets coming up from the village to worry his sheep. The eagle was in fact quite aggressive towards the falconer's spaniel, and so to clinch the permission to hawk rabbits the falconer enthused over his eagle's dog-chasing abilities.

Some days later he and the farmer set off to try for some rabbits, but in the first field a dog was seen hunting along a wall towards a bunch of frightened sheep. The excited farmer immediately demanded action from his new deterrent and so the eagle was slipped, with the falconer expecting it to pitch on a wall or on the ground. The eagle swept across the field, beating his mighty wings, then swooped low over the dog and bound-to the rump of one of the terrified sheep. Thus his permission to hawk was won and lost in a very short time!

Immature male gyr or jerkin

Time for hawking

Suitable land is the first priority for a falconer; even if there is plenty of the intended quarry there will be no hawking without it. Nevertheless, it is no good having land, hawks and quarry if the falconer has little or no time to dedicate to his sport. Flying long winged hawks is perhaps more time-consuming than flying a broad winged hawk at rabbits at weekends, but even broad winged hawks have to be housed, fed and attended to every day. Falconry cannot be a part-time sport.

Adult gyrfalcon

Acquiring skills

Having the land and the time does make it possible to practise falconry, but experience is also needed. Thus although the basic skills are not difficult to acquire, they cannot be learned overnight or fully absorbed in a week as a paying student. However good and well run falconry courses are, and a few are run to the very highest of standards, they are not the ideal way to learn the details and niceties of the art.

The skills and understanding needed to succeed at falconry in the field are best learned from an experienced falconer. This is not the only way; some have learned by trial and error, while others have grasped the basics from books, polishing their learning with practical experience in the field. Falconry has little room for those who only have a casual interest in the sport; such people do no good either for the sport or the hawks. A boy who is sent off by hopeful parents to learn all about falconry in a week, perhaps because they can think of nothing better to do with him in the school holidays, is not the best of young entries to the sport. In contrast, a young man who is determined enough to contact an experienced falconer will, by his very perseverence, prove his enthusiasm. The falconer will soon be able to see what potential the novice has as a falconer, and the novice will learn a great deal by example. When the time is ripe, no doubt the falconer will help the young novice to obtain his first hawk.

Obtaining hawks

These days hawks are freely available from captive breeding projects. Modern successes in captive breeding (the first peregrines were bred in England as recently as 1976) have certainly increased the supply of hawks available to falconers. All of the species of interest to the practical falconer now breed in captivity. Perhaps they are too freely available; in commercial breeding farms the selection of a potential customer is more likely to be influenced by his cheque book than by his experience. Of course, many of the commercial breeders do their very best to make sure that their hawks only go to suitable clients, but if their livelihood depends upon it, money might well overrule other considerations eventually. Of course, many falconers breed hawks in captivity, and most of them are more than generous in passing hawks on to carefully selected friends, acquaintances or protégés who have shown that they are likely to do the particular hawk justice.

Immature peregrine tiercel

Hawks from the wild

At the present time, nearly all species of birds of prey are once more breeding in the wild in Britain in increasing numbers. Peregrines are possibly more numerous than ever before, and sparrowhawks, kestrels and buzzards are also common. Goshawks are once again so prevalent in Europe that they are legally shot or trapped every year in the interests of game conservation. Nevertheless, in Britain it is difficult to obtain permission to import a wild-taken goshawk, and almost impossible to take a peregrine from the wild. It is hard to understand why this should be the case. There is no reason for refusing this permission on the grounds of conservation; a small cull would hardly affect wild population numbers. It is perfectly possible to meet all reasonable demands for hawks from captive breeding projects, and no doubt the commercial breeders rub their hands in glee, realising that they are the main source of supply and that a number of potential customers are being forced to their doors. It does seem unreasonable to make it all but impossible for a falconer to enjoy the excitement and thrill of getting his hawk from the wild.

Adult peregrine tiercel

Displays and exhibitions

In recent years falconry has become almost fashionable, with the dramatic increase in Falconry Club membership alone illustrating the current interest in the ancient sport. Certainly at least some of this interest has been cultivated by the many public appearances of trained falcons and hawks at game fairs and county shows. Of course these are not displays of falconry, because falconry is flying hawks at quarry, and many practical falconers disapprove of such performances. The hawks used in these performances are mainly just there for display, and few if any of them ever take quarry even if they are given a rare opportunity to do so. However, these displays do show trained hawks at close quarters, usually being flown to the lure. Many of these display hawks are kept in excellent condition, perform well to the lure and are a credit to their owners, although no doubt their potential as a falconer's hawk is well below par. The better managed the display, the easier the whole performance appears to be, and despite the accompanying commentary that clearly describes the problems and difficulties involved in keeping and training a hawk, this often encourages the idea that falconry is simple. After all, you only need to have a week or two of schooling, then you can buy a hawk, the necessary furniture and a training manual and hey presto you are a falconer!

Displays and exhibitions have done a great deal of good in years gone by in encouraging a more enlightened attitude towards birds of prey on the part of gamekeepers and landowners. They certainly 'pull' crowds to game fairs, and so help to boost the takings. However, the practice has also led to an increase in 'casual' falconry, which can only be bad falconry. A casual interest does not produce the sort of dedication that falconry demands to achieve success. Far more hawks are kept than are ever flown, and they rarely take quarry regularly. A casual interest leads to attempted short cuts to success, such that all of the real skills and details are cut out and training is reduced. This can in turn result in the would-be falconer chasing all over the countryside with a telemetry unit, trying to locate his lost hawk. Display flying also encourages the idea in some minds that flying to a lure *is* falconry, and that proper hawking at quarry is an unnecessary trimming. For a hawk or falcon whose whole evolution has been directed towards dramatically and wholeheartedly perfecting the techniques of hunting and taking quarry, to be reduced to a sort of living model aircraft, swooping and turning at the whim of an exhibitionist, is a prostitution of one of nature's finest achievements.

Success and failure

Falconry should be practised in a sporting manner. Over many years a fine see-saw balance has been established between hawk and quarry in many of the traditional flights. Whether it is a peregrine stooping on a grouse or a sparrowhawk chasing a blackbird, the balance is such that the good hawk and the experienced falconer will succeed on several occasions, while the bad hawk and the moderate falconer will usually fail. There would be little satisfaction or sportsmanship to be had if the scales were tipped too much in favour of the hawk and the falconer, while equally there would be little point in going out hawking always to fail at quarry.

Lanner falcon

In the old days a cast or pair of hawks was generally flown at herons or kites because, alternating their stoops, the hawks could hopefully keep the quarry from climbing too high or going too far. However, in the majority of flights today only a single hawk is flown. While a cast of hawks is normally more than a match for the average rook, with the smaller gulls a cast is often needed to get the balance right and to give the falconer some hope of success sufficiently near for him to be able to enjoy the flight. The cunning of the magpie demands the help of a second hawk, and late in the season a merlin might well be glad of assistance with a high-ringing lark. In greyhound coursing it can easily be observed that a pair of greyhounds is well matched to the average hare. However, if a third hound gets loose and joins in the course the hare is easily killed, and under the rules of coursing the owner of the loose dog is fined. Thus it is important always to give the quarry a sporting chance.

It might be thought that it is unsporting to fly a very large hawk such as a gyrfalcon at a partridge or grouse. However, a large hawk which has great strength and speed is often less nimble than her quarry, and so is handicapped by her lack of manoeuvrability.

I prefer not to fly hybrid hawks but to use the best of what nature has provided and to depend upon my own attempts at skilful management. There is little satisfaction to be had in producing a hawk that flies high and fast if that only upsets the balance between hawk and quarry. The reward in hawking must surely come from making the most of what nature offers you and seeking out the individual skills, ability and potential of every hawk that comes into your hands. Yet it may well be that falconry will change, since for the first time in the long and honourable history of this ancient art, science is beginning to play a big part, with selective breeding and hybridisation replacing hard-won skills.

Telemetry

Perhaps the greatest influence on modern hawking after the advent of captive breeding is the use and abuse of radio-tracking telemetry. If used as a supplement to the traditional, time-honoured methods of following up a lost hawk, then telemetry is a wonderful aid, and it has assisted in the recovery of many a hawk that might otherwise have been lost. However, all too often the radio is thought of as a sort of magic formula that allows the falconer to fly his hawk in unsuitable country, or when she is not in proper flying condition, and to cut short her training. Over-reliance on the device encourages many falconers to become careless of the balance that must be maintained between hunger and disobedience. It is a sad and disappointing sight to see a falconer wandering around with the receiver and aerial permanently at the ready, not really knowing whether his hawk is flying at quarry or just soaring. The whole point of falconry is to be able to see your hawk in action at quarry, to be able to watch most, if not all, of the flight, and to easily recover the hawk whether or not she has killed. If you become too dependent on telemetry, you will fly the hawk whatever its condition, knowing that with the radio you have an excellent chance of recovering her should she wander away or kill at a great distance. You will also be tempted to fly the hawk in unsuitable country, confident that the radio will balance the odds against you irrespective of whether or not you see a good flight. It can be very satisfying *not* to have to use the hawk radio throughout the whole of the hawking season.

Adult saker – pale phase

Good practice

It is right to feel proud about catching quarry which is worthy of the hawk being flown. However, there is not much sport to be had in catching a hand-reared, barely full-grown partridge or pheasant early on in the season. Similarly, game that has been reared recently in captivity and 'turned down' (released into the wild) should also be avoided. Similarly, while it is legitimate to hunt a grouse or rook out of cover two, three or even four times if necessary when entering a young hawk, or to reward a hawk that has been disappointed on a few occasions, to continually hound any quarry that has beaten you fairly is of little credit to you or to your hawk. One or two good flights and kills in a day is enough per hawk, particularly where the quarry cannot be supplemented by a rearing programme. It is surely more satisfying and sporting to enjoy quality flights rather than to be concerned solely with the quantity killed. Of course, quality hawking will invariably produce quarry in the bag, but even the best of hawks can only kill if quarry is available. Catching yet another grouse, rook or rabbit just for the sake of adding it to the bag, is not something to shout about.

Although success in the field is one way in which the experience and ability of a falconer can be measured, he should not have to prove himself to others with fancy scores, since all sportsmen have their share of successes and failures. What is important is that the hawk should be trained and flown well and in a sporting manner. Hawking late in the day should be avoided; game in particular are easily caught just before dark and the hawk will fly aggressively, not because of skilled training and management, but because she begins to doubt if she will feed that day. Grouse are probably troubled very little by being scattered in the evening, but it is better that the landowner or the keeper should see their tenants coming off the moor at a sensible hour, satisfied and hopefully successful, rather than see them stay out until dark, determined at all costs to get the most out of hawk, dog and moorland.

Whether you are hawking on field or moor, quarry should be wild and should always be offered a sporting chance. Although it is used in other countries, bagged quarry is fortunately illegal in Britain as well as being against the code of conduct of the British Falconers' Club. The very idea of releasing quarry is against both the spirit and the traditions of falconry and sportsmanship. A falconer who finds it necessary to use such methods to train his hawks will look like a very poor falconer beside the man who succeeds in the field without resort to any dubious practices.

The responsibilities of the falconer

It should never be forgotten that all too often field sports are judged by the worst examples of their kind. For example, of the many hundreds of peregrines in captivity in this country, only perhaps ten per cent are flown regularly at quarry. Far too many are kept as status symbols, or are exhibited for financial gain. Unfortunately, hawk-keepers, exhibitionists and circus performers all masquerade under the title of 'falconer', which does little to help maintain the proper image and respectability that the sport deserves. For falconry to continue to be acceptable it is necessary to maintain the highest standards possible, both in hawk management and performance and in success in the field. Fortunately, there are still a few practitioners who continue to maintain these high standards.

Today, the majority of falconers train and fly their own hawks. In earlier times the giants of falconry such as Fisher, Lascelles and Blaine, although fully capable of training and flying a hawk, all employed professional falconers to help with this task. Thus the modern falconer reaps a greater satisfaction from doing it all for himself. To succeed in such a difficult and time-consuming art is very rewarding, but success also carries with it the great responsibility of ensuring the survival of a noble, simple and satisfying pastime.

Adult saker – dark phase

1

The hawk house, shelters and weathering ground

The hawk house

Long before a hawk is obtained it is necessary to give some thought, effort and money to provide a suitable hawk house or shelter to ensure the comfort, security and wellbeing of its proposed inmate. If one considers the trouble and expense that is usually involved in acquiring the hawk of one's choice, it is often surprising to find how meanly or indeed, badly it is housed.

In many older properties there is usually a stable or outbuilding that can be adapted to serve as an ideal mews or hawk house, provided it is not too damp and has been or can be altered to have suitable ventilation. Even in many modern properties, the garage (which so often occupies the greatest area of floor space) or the utility room can be acquired and partitioned off to a suitable size for the purpose. One falconer, on having a modern house built, had a brick extension erected behind his garage, adding little to the overall building cost but providing a dry and sound mews. A roomy garden shed, solidly constructed of wood, can also be adapted, but if the floor is wooden it is better raised a foot or so above the ground on brick or concrete block piers.

Doors and windows

However the hawks are to be kept within the hawk house, whether tied to a perch or loose, it is necessary to have double doors at the entrance, either in the form of a porch or, even better, with a small outer room. A hawk is easily lost through a single door. Windows or openings are necessary to enable the building to be well aired but these should have perpendicular bars of wood, bamboo or, better, iron spaced not more than 1¾in (4cm) apart completely covering them on the inside. For additional security it is a good plan to cover the outside of the window with ½in (1.25cm) wire mesh or weld mesh. An unprotected or open window can result in the loss of a hawk as easily as an open door. The Old Hawking Club lost one of their finest haggard peregrines, 'Dawn', in the spring of 1922, when she got out through a partially opened window in her moulting room. It is also necessary to have shutters to the windows so that the room can be completely blacked out.

The floor

The floor of my mews is covered with quarry tiles and ideally it would have been better if the walls could also have been tiled to a height of about 3 or 4ft (1m). With a tiled floor and walls it is far easier to wipe up any mutes and, on a nice sunny day, when the building is scrubbed out with disinfectant the tiles dry rather more quickly than does a concrete floor. The floor is best covered with a good thick layer of dry sand from which the mutes and castings can be scooped up each day. Some falconers spread newspapers beneath the perch and change them daily. It is advisable to weigh the paper down with iron rods. Sand is also suitable if the hawk is loose in the mews or is on a low perch. With a high 'screen' perch, sawdust or shavings could be used instead of sand.

Dimensions and accessories

Ideally, the room should be at least 7ft (2m) high, so that there is plenty of head room should a screen perch be used. It is also better not to have beams, ledges or shelves above the level of any perch, as these may encourage a hawk to bate continually, jumping in an attempt to reach a higher resting place.

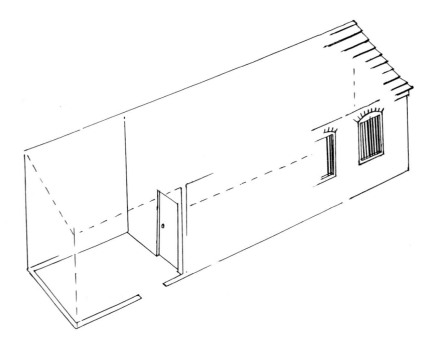

Fig. 1 A lean-to building with an outer room, suitable for use as a hawk house

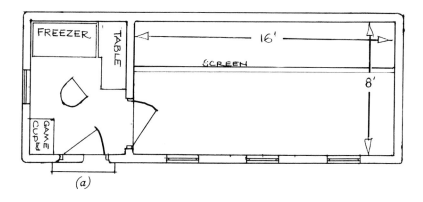

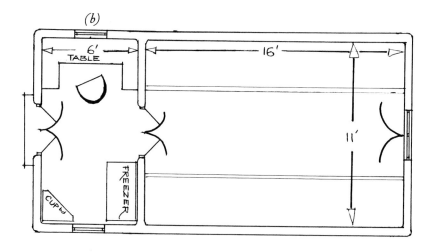

Fig. 2 Two plans of mews: (a) with a single screen perch and an outer room and (b) with a double screen perch

It is better that hawk hoods and gloves, etc. are not hung in the mews proper but are kept in the outer room or porch. If an outer room is available, it is convenient to furnish it with a table and chair and perhaps a cupboard. Pegs on which to hang hoods, gloves and lures can be arranged on the wall. It is better if hoods are not hung on nails or cup hooks which, particularly with Anglo-Indian hoods, have a tendency to pull them out of shape. It is better to make up a simple board through which heavy dowling rod may be glued, thus forming neat little pegs.

If the room is large enough it can also house a freezer, and an old fashioned meat cupboard covered in perforated zinc is a useful addition in which defrosting meat and fresh food can be kept free from flies. Gloves are also better for being hung up away from the attentions of mice who seem to find the meat-stained leather particularly attractive. The scales used to weigh your hawk can be set up ready for use on the table or a convenient shelf and the cupboard can be used to house the few simple tools and medications you may require. An electrical supply is an advantage for lighting and for the freezer unit and a simple heater, such as the tube heaters used to heat glasshouses, is a useful addition to dry out the mews properly in damp weather while the hawks are out on the weathering lawn.

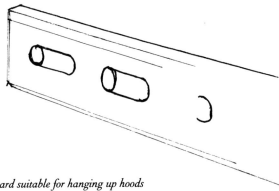

Fig. 3 A board suitable for hanging up hoods

The perch

Traditionally, hawks are kept tied to a screen or high perch when in the hawk house. The perch should run the length of the room, about 4ft (1.2m) from the back wall, allowing a further 6ft (2m) or so in front for easy passage. The pole should be at about shoulder height or a little less (4ft 6in (1.37m)), a convenient height for the falconer to reach comfortably but high enough for an unhooded hawk to feel secure, her head being about the level of the falconer's face. If the room is wide, 14ft (4m) or so, it is sensible to have a screen running down both sides of the room, at exactly the same height.

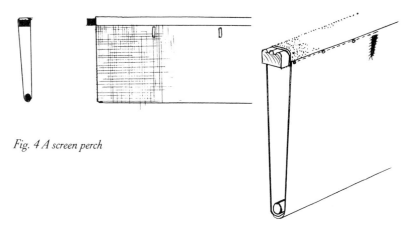

Fig. 4 A screen perch

Fig. 5 A screen perch showing a hessian screen
nailed to either side of the perch. The pipe in
the bottom of the screen helps to keep it taut

When on the screen the distance between hawks is determined by
how each is tied up, the species and therefore the size of the various
hawks and their attitude to each other. Some species of hawk frighten
others; some individual hawks are aggressive, even to others of their
own species. 'Jallad', a haggard peregrine that I had for some seventeen
years, was extremely frightened by the presence of a goshawk. A Red-
tail buzzard had the same effect on her. It is preferable to house
goshawks or broad winged hawks in a separate hawk house away from
any long wings. For larger hawks, peregrines, lanners, etc., a distance of
2ft (60cm) between hawks and 3ft (1m) from the end wall would serve.
For larger goshawks, Red-tail buzzards, etc., the distance between them
should be a minimum of 3ft (1m).

The actual screen should hang from both sides of the perch, not as a
single screen from under the pole. The screen is best made from a length
of hessian, and if bought of sufficient width (available about 4ft 6in
(1.37m) wide and in a variety of colours), it can be hung so as to form a
sling, in which can be laid a heavy pole or a length of iron piping so that
the hessian is kept taut. This gives a hawk more support should she bate
from the perch and need to clamber back up the screen. The edges of the
hessian can be tacked with carpet tacks direct to either side of the perch
or, alternatively, if the perch is to be covered with carpet or a similar
material the screen can be sewn to the carpet before it is slid on to the
perch to form a roller towel. It will then require a small number of tacks
to keep the carpet on the top of the perch. Holes should be cut (at the
appropriate distance apart) through both sides of the screen through
which the leashes can be tied. These holes can be bound or stitched
around the edges. A screen should hang at least 2ft 3in (69cm) below
the pole.

The surface of the perch is of great importance as a trained hawk spends many hours tied thereon. For long winged hawks the surface should be as wide as possible without risk of fouling the perch or screen with their mutes. For peregrines or gyrs the perch can be at least a comfortable 4in (10cm) wide, but 2½–3in (6½–7cm) would be better for sakers, lanners or lugger falcons. Of course, for the tiny merlin 1½–2in (4cm) is more suitable. For broad winged hawks, goshawks or sparrowhawks a natural pole is convenient.

Although long winged hawks prefer to sit on a shelf-like perch it is an advantage to make the surface of the perch somewhat irregular so that the point of pressure on the hawk's foot is changed as it moves position. My own perches have strips of rounded wood glued and nailed to the surface. An alternative would be to gouge out two or three grooves the entire length of the perch.

Fig. 6 A selection of perch surfaces

I cover the surface with tightly stretched old lorry inner tube. This makes both a comfortable and a hygienic surface that can easily be wiped clean with a suitable disinfectant. Some falconers prefer to give their hawks a choice of surface. Proper wool carpet, not nylon, is a comfortable perch and should be pile side up. J. G. Mavrogordato used to offer his hawks the choice of carpet to one side and a piece of roughened sandstone to the other side, the stone cunningly recessed into the surface of the perch. Today many falconers use 'Astro-turf' as a perch surface.

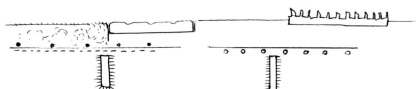

Fig. 7 A screen perch surfaced with carpet, stone, rubber or Astro-turf

Whatever is used it is important to ensure that the jesses cannot get caught up on any projecting piece and that the hand can be run along the perch without catching. If properly used, the screen perch is an excellent and secure way to house hawks at night. However, it is important to make sure that any hawk being put on a screen is fit and healthy and understands how to climb back up the screen on to the perch should she bate off. To this end it is a wise practice always to watch a new hawk until she shows that she is capable of regaining the perch.

Some falconers, probably because they wish to give their hawk more freedom of movement, give the hawk an extra length of leash on the screen. Although apparently a kind idea, it will in fact make it rather more difficult for a hawk to regain the perch should she bate off and will also make it necessary to tie hawks further apart.

The hawk house should be 'blacked out' with the shutters provided when any but the very tamest of hawks are on the screen. With proper management trained hawks will normally spend most of their day out 'weathering' on their 'block' or bow perch in the fresh air of the garden and so should not spend more time than is necessary in the darkness of the mews.

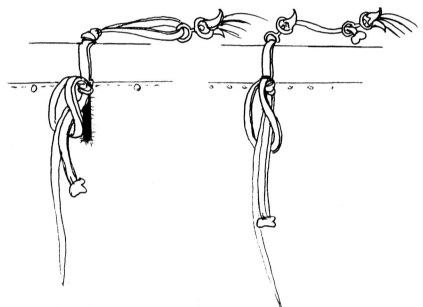

Fig. 8 Two methods of extending the amount of movement a hawk is allowed when tied to the screen

Alternative indoor perches

Alternatively, hawks can be housed indoors on 'block' perches or bow/ring perches adapted for indoor use with a lead or board base set down on the floor of the building. This requires a much larger floor area per hawk, approximately 6ft × 6ft (2m × 2m). There should be no beams or ledges showing to tempt the hawk to a higher perch. When in use the hawk house is better 'blacked-out' until the hawk or hawks become very tame and well mannered. The floor should be covered with at least 4in (10cm) of sand to soak up any mutes and to cushion the wing feathers and feet should the hawk bate. *See* indoor perches, pages 33 and 39.

Another type of indoor perch which I saw in use with both long and short winged hawks in Canada is the shelf perch. This shelf can be fitted into the corner of the room or can be a length of shelf along a wall. Although the majority of shelf perches I saw were about 2ft (60cm) above the floor, some were as high as 4ft (1m) or so. The leash is tied to a ring attached to the wall or floor under the shelf. There is little point in tying the leash to the ring with a lot of slack; it is better that the leash is of such a length to allow the hawk to perch comfortably anywhere on her shelf but no more. Once again, the floor should be liberally covered with clean sand and the mutes and castings should be cleared up each day.

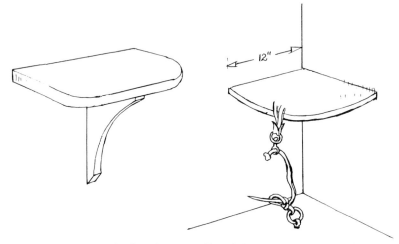

Fig. 9 A shelf perch covered with wool carpet or Astro-turf

Fig. 10 A corner shelf perch about 2 ft (61 cm) above the floor

Shelters

An alternative to housing hawks in an enclosed building at night is to construct a roofed shelter under which they can perch, protected from wind and rain but having the advantages of fresh air and light. Only trained hawks should be housed in this way. An untrained hawk, and many hawks caught in the wild, would continually bate in such a shelter. While they might eventually 'bate' themselves into submitting to such treatment that is hardly the way to cultivate a good relationship between falconer and hawk. Personally, I do not like the idea of having my hawks so close to the dew-damp ground throughout the night and at some small risk of straddling a block or even getting loose. To guard against a lost hawk it it better to fence in the front of the building with netting, which hopefully would also keep out inquisitive cats, dogs, foxes or rats. The floor should be well drained with a thick layer of gravel topped with sand.

Rather simpler to construct would be individual shelters, the first of which I saw in use by Phillip Glasier in the 1950s. Certainly they have much to recommend them as housing for such birds as goshawks which are not always safe near to others and might well do much damage should they get loose. Enclosed in their own pen they are safe. It is important in constructing such pens to ensure that they are of sufficient size so that a bating hawk cannot reach the netting with outstretched wings. It is convenient to build such a shelter against an existing wall or fence, preferably protecting the inhabitant from the prevailing wind. Although many such shelters as these are used as nighttime housing they are better used only as weathering daytime shelters. They are particularly convenient if the falconer is away much of the day.

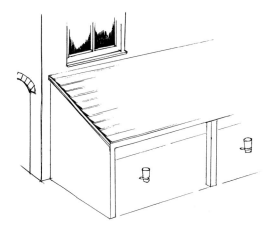

Fig. 11 A permanent shelter for a number of hawks which is built against the wall of a house

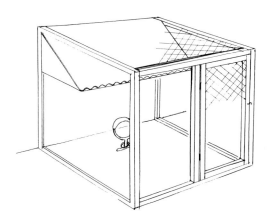

Fig. 12 An individual shelter, partially roofed and built against an existing fence or wall

27

A further shelter I saw in use in Norfolk some years ago provided welcome shade for a gyrfalcon. Built of tubular aluminium, with marine plyboard riveted on as roof and back, it provided a very portable shelter that could be moved about the weathering lawn. It is necessary to make the shelter sufficiently large so that a restless hawk cannot get entangled around the uprights. The illustration shows an alternative design. In this pattern it is important to make the base arms sufficiently long to make the whole screen stable.

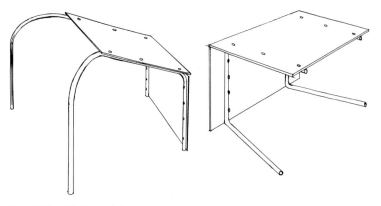

Fig. 13 Portable lawn shelters

Weathering ground

For much of the day a trained hawk should be out in the fresh air on the weathering lawn. All hawks enjoy early morning and winter sunlight, but are better in the shade in strong summer sun. Hawks seem to enjoy light rain and drizzle, but in heavy rain or storms they are better under shelters or in the hawk house.

The lawn should be sheltered from the prevailing wind by a garden wall, a fence or substantial hedge. Ideally, there should be a tree or two to provide shade in hot weather. Ash, oak or sycamore produce a nice dappled shade. Large apple trees also serve well, but in season are prone to drop Newton inspiring missiles on to an unsuspecting hawk below. If you have dog- or cat-owning neighbours or live in fox country, it is better to ring-fence the lawn with chicken netting. Beware also of game cocks, turkeys and peafowl, all of which can create havoc on hawk lawns. Swans and Canada geese have invaded my weathering lawn, fortunately causing no damage, and recently we have been concerned about the damage mink might do. Certainly, cats are a danger and as long ago as 1879 The Old Hawking Club had two fine hawks attacked by a cat at Fermoy in Co. Cork. Both hawks, a fine magpie tiercel,

'Buccaneer', and a falcon, 'Galatea', died of blood poisoning. Recently there have been a few cases where foxes have been suspected as the culprits.

The lawn should be of sufficient size to enable perches to be moved to fresh ground each day. The grass should be kept mown but in very dry weather it is better to leave the grass rather longer than usual. This will protect the wing tips and feet of your hawk from too vigorous a contact with the baked ground.

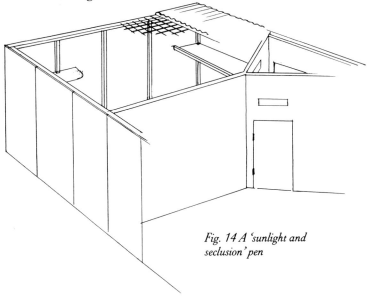

Fig. 14 A 'sunlight and seclusion' pen

'Sunlight and seclusion' pen

Instead of keeping your hawks in a mews, shelter or on a lawn it is possible to keep them loose in a 'sunlight and seclusion' pen. This design of pen has been developed by those falconers who have put much time, effort and thought into the breeding of birds of prey in captivity. Most hawks seem to settle down very well in these enclosures. They are free to enjoy sunlight, rain or shade and shelter at will. In the past falconers have kept merlins free in a room, taking them out to fly them, and there is no why one shouldn't do so with any species of hawk. Certainly, such a pen is an ideal way to house a hawk at night. She could be taken up each morning and could spend the day on the lawn. I kept a gyrfalcon this way for some years as she was never to be entirely trusted on the screen perch. If hawks are housed like this in the flying season, it is better that they are fed on the fist rather than being allowed to feed themselves.

These same pens are ideal for moulting your hawks: two, three or even four compatible hawks will happily share the same pen. If the

The hawk house

falconer is away, any reliable person can safely slide the daily rations down the feed shute. Plastic drainpipes make ideal shutes, although my brother once suggested that they might encourage hawks to fly around looking for drainpipes in expectation of food! The pipe should be so positioned that the food is deposited under the protection of the nesting shelf (see diagrams) so that the food cannot be muted upon. Of course, any game hawks or others that are not required for hawking in the spring, can be paired and housed in such pens for breeding purposes.

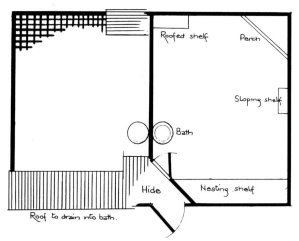

Fig. 15 A plan for a pair of 'sunlight and seclusion' pens. The pens measure 16 ft × 12 ft (5 m × 3.5 m approx.) and the nesting shelf is 2 ft (61 cm) wide

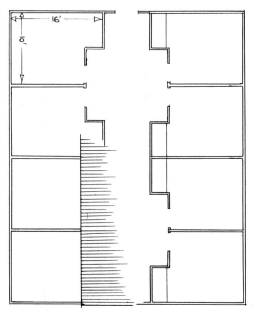

Fig. 16 A plan for a group of eight breeding pens. Each pen measures 16 ft × 10 ft (5 m × 3 m approx.)

Baths

Whether your hawks are to be kept in pens, shelters or on the hawk lawn, a regular bath is necessary for well kept plumage. In breeding pens it is better to have a built-in concrete bath, ideally with a drainage system and a supply pipe so that the bath water can be changed without entering the pen. The bath should measure at least 3ft (90cm) in circumference.

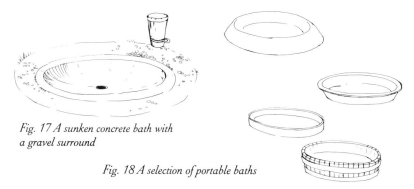

Fig. 17 A sunken concrete bath with a gravel surround

Fig. 18 A selection of portable baths

The sides should slope in to give a maximum depth of 6in (15cm) of water. A similar bath can be constructed on the weathering lawn, but although a shy hawk will invariably enter such a sunken bath more readily than she will a portable bath, a permanent bath is more difficult to keep clean. In addition, whether in a pen or on the lawn, it is advisable to surround the bath with a bed of pea-gravel or sand so that it does not get too muddy. In a breeding pen the bath can be positioned in such a way that rain water from the roofed areas runs down a pipe into the bath and so replenishes the supply. Through overflowing in heavy rain the dirty water is flushed out and at least partially replaced.

Portable baths are now available in a variety of designs. Custom-made ones are usually moulded in fibreglass which is light in weight and easy to keep clean. Cream pans, often made in stainless steel, are also suitable and the lid of a large plastic or rubber dustbin can be used, too. With a dustbin lid it is better to cut off the handle with a hacksaw so that it will sit flat on the ground.

When on the weathering lawn a hawk should not be left too long with the bath. She will foul the water with her mutes. It is better to offer the bath only every second or third day so that the hawk will have a thorough soaking. Some hawks, if offered a bath every day, will do little more than wet their legs, then hop out again. Some hawks, however, do require a bath every day. A very good peregrine of mine who has shown excellent sport at grouse for many seasons now, will, if she doesn't have a bath in the morning while weathering, go off the minute she is flown over a point to find a puddle or burn in which to bathe.

Block perches

Long winged hawks are normally tied to a 'block' on the weathering lawn. The simplest block is a length of wood with a spike set in the centre of the base and a large staple knocked into the top or side of the block. A staple easily works loose and pulls out. Indeed, with the staple as a fixture in the side of the block the hawk quickly becomes entangled with the leash winding around the base as she turns about. With the staple in the top the falcon is not so easily entangled, but if she bates the leash is at such an angle that it pulls up through the tail feathers, so damaging the tail.

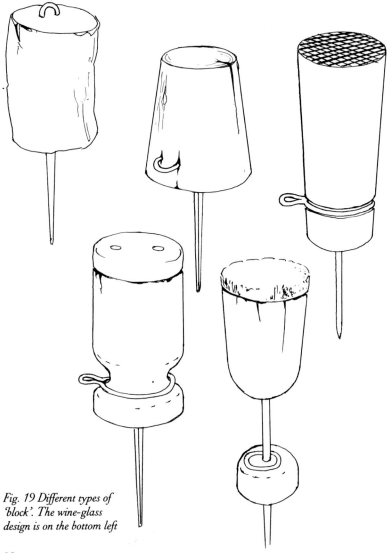

Fig. 19 Different types of 'block'. The wine-glass design is on the bottom left

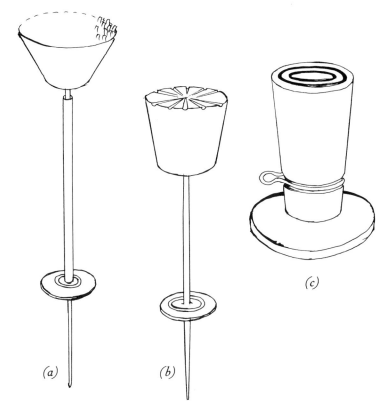

Fig. 20 (a) A high block with an aluminium sleeve around the spike. (b) A design which allows the leash to tangle around the spike. (c) An indoor block with a heavy lead base

To reduce these risks various designs of block were developed with a swivelling ring so that however much the hawk turned about the leash would pull straight if she bated. However, time has shown up the weaknesses in the various ideas. A ring let into a narrow groove around the block works well until the wood swells from the damp and the ring jams tight. If the groove is eased a little, there is then some risk of the leash sticking between the groove and the iron ring. An alternative is to have a ring or a figure-of-eight shaped double ring swivelling loosely around a metal spike, with the wooden block mounted above and a wooden block or metal plate fixed below the tie ring. With this design the leash has a tendency to wrap around the spike as the hawk turns and does not easily pull straight again. To overcome this some falconers slip a loose aluminium pipe over the stem of the block which allows a wrapped leash to pull straight. Over many years I have found that a very free-running ring about the neck of a wine glass shaped block to be as near foolproof as possible. With any block where iron runs against wood it is worth while to grease well on occasion.

The hawk house

Some falconers use high blocks, believing that their hawk will be more content well above the ground. However, I feel there is a much greater risk of a hawk hanging on such a block, particularly if the top of the block is anything other than absolutely smooth. This reduces the risk of the leash catching over the block top. All too often these tall blocks have a cork top or, even worse, an Astro-turf surface, which although ideal for the hawk to perch on snags the leash all too easily. For safe and secure 'weathering' I have yet to find anything better than the 'hour glass' or 'wine glass' style shown in the illustrations.

'Nimran' on an Astro-turf covered block

With a block 1ft (30cm) or so in height there is little danger of the leash catching over the top of the perch. Therefore, the top can be 'dressed' with the surface of your choice. Colonel Blaine always used cork, maintaining that it dried out more quickly after rain. Many hawks seem to appreciate the springy surface of Astro-turf (you can buy an Astro-turf door mat and cut it to shape with a Stanley knife or scissors) which can be glued or tacked on. Other falconers of experience, such as Jack Mavrogordato, believed in using natural stone tops. Sandstone is easily cut into a rough shape with an ordinary wood saw (it will probably need to be resharpened), then shaped and rounded up with a surf-form or heavy blacksmith's rasp. For many years I made up such tops, leaving the surface somewhat irregular, and fastened them to the blocks with countersunk brass screws, after drilling holes with a suitably sized masonry drill.

It has been suggested that a concrete top will serve as well as stone. Concrete is more likely to chip or break than stone and the surface is rather abrasive. The top of a block, if left as plain wood, can be grooved or channelled in a variety of ways. Such grooving produces an irregular surface, suitable for the hawk, but some designs may hinder the quick draining of the block top after rain. Plain, smooth wooden tops are certainly the safest surface and the easiest to keep clean. Some falconers paint their blocks but there is a risk of flaking paint getting on to the hawk food. If varnished with a good yacht varnish, then wax polished occasionally, your blocks should last many years.

Peregrine tiercel half-way through the moult on a stone block

Immature peregrine falcon on a wooden block

Rings

The ring to which the leash is tied on the block should be made from ¼in (6mm) iron rod, so that it will not pull out of shape, and it should be professionally welded.

With certain designs of block there is a risk of a lost hawk should the wooden block pull off the spike. To guard against this have a plate, rather larger than the tie ring, welded to the spike. The wooden block can then be attached with screws. Ordinarily the spikes should be 'jagged' by the blacksmith before they are driven into the prepared hole in the base of the block. This will ensure that they do not come out.

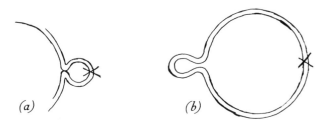

Fig. 21 Rings for blocks. It is better to weld at point X on (b) rather than point X on (a)

Fig. 22 (a) A block spike which has been 'jagged' or notched to ensure that it holds fast in the wooden block. (b) A metal plate welded to the top of a spike

Things to avoid in block design

Over the years falconers have devised blocks from 5ft (1.5m) high to little more than molehills. Some have swivelling tops, others have swivelling stems. However, do avoid the following:

    any form of platform top, such as an Arab perch

    any block that is sharply tapered

    too small a circumference to the block top.

With any one of the above faults it is far too easy for a hawk to straddle the block, not only ruffling or breaking its tail feathers, but also making it extremely difficult to untangle.

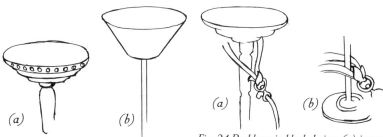

Fig. 23 (a) An Arab-type block. (b) A sharply tapered block

Fig. 24 Problems in block design: (a) jesses straddling the top of a block; (b) a hawk trapped by 'straddled' jesses against the spike of a block; (c) (below, left) a hawk 'hanging' over a high block

Too large a block means that it is liable to be fouled by the hawk muting. A block that is too high catches the wind, so tempting the hawk to bate. There is also more risk of a hawk hanging over the block. A block that is too low is unattractive to the hawk and her tail will touch wet grass or mutes.

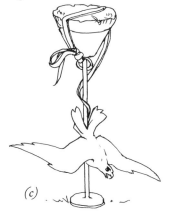

Goshawk on a traditional bow perch

Bow and ring perches

Bow and ring perches are normally used for short winged and broad winged hawks. The ring to which the leash is tied should be large enough to run easily over the bow and over any padding there may be. A bow can be made from a length of ash wood. Either steam it or soak it in boiling water before attempting to bend it. Keep it in shape with a length of wire across the circumference, not forgetting to put a ring on to the bow. Far longer lasting is an iron bow made up by the local blacksmith. An iron bow will need a strip of wood riveted to it, or a length of plastic water pipe can be slipped on while it is being made up.

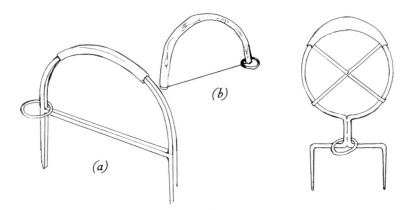

Fig. 25 Bow perches made of iron (a) and ash (b)   *Fig. 26 A ring perch*

A rather more portable and practical idea is the ring perch. As the tie ring does not travel over the bow, the top of the ring can be covered with strong leather (buckskin is ideal) or rubber to form a padded perch. The ring to which the hawk leash is tied encircles the neck of the perch. There is some risk of the leash wrapping round and round the neck on top of the ring. This can be helped by using a stiffish leash of Terylene cord rather than flat nylon or leather. It is important with a ring perch to fill in the ring of the perch with a canvas screen or with crossed leather or metal. If left open, the hawk might go through the ring and so become entangled.

For a sparrowhawk an excellent bow perch can be made up from a length of plastic water pipe (¾in (19mm) mains pipe, not hose pipe) which can be glued and riveted either on to a metal base or to a board as a portable indoor or car perch.

Fig. 27 A simple sparrowhawk bow perch made from a length of plastic water pipe

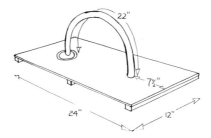

Fig. 28 A portable sparrowhawk perch

Temporary 'blocks'

For temporary 'blocks' large flower pots can be used. All that you need are some strong iron spikes with a ring formed at the top. An upturned flower pot can be stood over each spike after you have threaded the hawk leash through the hole in the base of the pot and tied it to the ring.

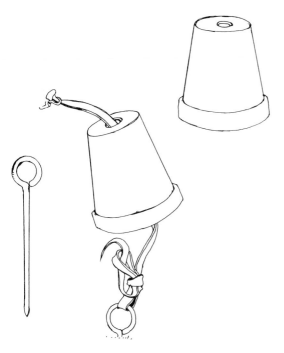

Fig. 29 A temporary flower pot 'block' perch

2
Falconry furniture

Gloves

In the West it is the normal practice to carry your hawk on your left hand. However, if you are left-handed there is no reason why you should not carry your hawk on the right fist as did Colonel Blaine and his one time falconer, Leonard Potter. Patrick Morel, the eminent Belgium falconer, does so today.

Strong leather gardening gloves do very well and are cheap to buy, particularly if a right- and a left-handed falconer can buy a pair between them. However, most falconers prefer to buy a custom-made hawking glove. The suppliers listed on page 238 all produce well-made gloves.

For a goshawk or a Red-tail buzzard the glove needs to be of moderately thick but flexible leather. It is normal practice to sew on a second layer of leather over the thumb, first two fingers and part of the body of the glove. The glove also has a reasonably long cuff, so protecting the forearm. It is traditional to trim the glove with a bound edge, often in a contrasting colour and with a tassle. This tassle can be used to hang up the glove out of reach of mice or dogs. Some falconers also like a leather loop or a brass 'D' sewn into the edge on to which they

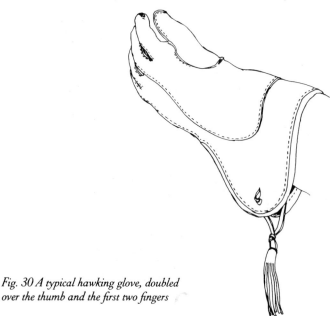

Fig. 30 A typical hawking glove, doubled over the thumb and the first two fingers

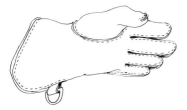

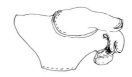

Fig. 31 A short cuffed, lightweight glove

Fig. 32 A two-fingered glove suitable for sparrowhawks or merlins

can tie the leash of any hawk they are carrying. This is a sensible idea when carrying a hawk on rough terrain or when asking a friendly amateur to carry a hawk for you. Other falconers sew all sorts of gadgets and clips to their gloves on which to attach swivels, Aylmeri jesses or even hoods. All are better put away in pockets where they are safe.

Many falconers prefer to use a much thinner glove if carrying a peregrine or a smaller hawk. Alternatively, the glove need only be a single layer of leather. For such hawks the glove can be made rather shorter in the cuff.

A third type of glove is occasionally used for carrying merlins or sparrowhawks. This glove only covers the thumb and first two fingers.

The author with a merlin on a special merlin glove

Leather

The best possible leather now available for glove making is deerskin (buckskin). It is both supple enough and extremely strong. Dogskin was also used in the past: it has no sweat pores. However, other than the occasional piece of 'dingo' skin it is no longer available. Normally, a hawking glove is made 'sueded' or flesh-side out. This makes a comfortable perch and is not slippery, but is easy for the hawk to grip. However, some falconers order gloves with the smooth-side out.

If feeding a hawk a great deal on the glove, it quickly becomes soiled, particularly if using rather messy food such as recently thawed day-old chicks. If made from good quality buckskin, a glove can be scrubbed every now and again. Do not make it too wet and pull it back into shape before drying it slowly. It will be rather stiff on first drying, but after a day or two of use will supple up again.

However, it is a sound plan to change your glove fairly regularly. A new glove is very much cheaper than a new hawk. Although a glove should be sufficiently thick to protect the hand it is far more comfortable for both hawk and man only to have a glove which is just heavy enough for the purpose. It is much safer if the jesses can be 'felt' through the glove as they are then less likely to slip through the fingers.

Many falconers make up their own gloves. All that is required is suitable leather, a pattern, No. 1 gloving needles, No. 18 linen thread and some beeswax (*see* patterns, instructions and supplies at the end of this book).

Jesses

The traditional jess is cut in various sizes, shapes and thicknesses according to the species of hawk for which they are required (*see* patterns and measurements at the end of this book).

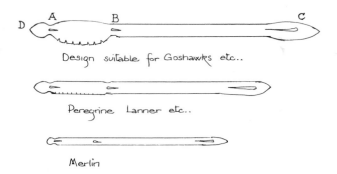

Fig. 33 Different types of jesse

Gloving buckskin makes excellent jesses. Kangaroo, calfskin and dogskin are also suitable. Before cutting a jess to its final shape, cut strips rather wider than you eventually need. Cut along the grain of the leather, that is parallel with the backbone of the animal. Grease the strips, or wet them and stretch them as much as you can. Finally, cut to the correct shape. The critical measurement is between the punched or rounded ends of the slits marked in the illustration below. It is this exact distance that establishes the correct fit.

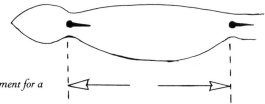

Fig. 34 The critical measurement for a correct fit

Fitting the jess

To put a jess on a hawk, wrap the leg part, A–B, around the leg of the hawk, below any identity ring she may carry. Push point D through the slit at B until slit A comes through; put point C through slit A and pull the jess through until the knot is tight. Artery forceps or strong tweezers are a great help when jessing up a hawk. It sounds difficult, but when repeated a few times it is straightforward. However, I remember once helping an experienced falconer to jess up a hawk. With glasses on the end of his nose he carefully recited, 'D through B, C through A, pull it tight' . . . and the jess fell off! You need to remember which letter goes where.

Alternatively, you can put point D through slit B and pull until the two slits A and B are in line. You then put point C through both slit B and A and again pull up tight. Some falconers consider that this method

Fig. 35 One method of putting on jesses

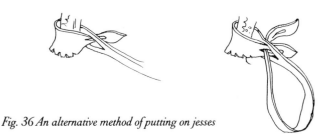

Fig. 36 An alternative method of putting on jesses

makes a neater knot, but as it turns in the edge of the leather it may be more likely to rub the leg of the hawk. Both knots, which are almost identical, are equally secure provided they are pulled up tight.

Fig. 37 Both methods when completed

To arrive at exactly the same knot as the second method you can prepare the jess by putting point D through slit B and then pulling the leg part of the jess right through before putting the jess around the leg of the hawk and proceeding as in method one above.

Fig. 38 A jess prepared for the method shown in Fig. 36

Whichever method you use, and all are correct if the old masters are anything to go by, you should end up with a snug fitting jess. It should not be tight but should easily swivel about the leg without leaving more than a little spare in the leg opening. Frederick II, writing in 1248, said of jesses:

From a piece of soft but tough leather are cut two equal strips the length of one's hand and about the width of a man's little finger ... It is best to place the leather strip about the falcon's leg and measure accurately the distance between these two slits. The perforated end [slit A] is now drawn through the second slit [slit B] until the first perforation has passed through the opening; then the narrower, longer, unperforated portion of the jess [point C] is picked up and inserted in the first slit [slit A] ... In adjusting the two jesses to the falcon's legs, the upper edge of each jess should be drawn a little tighter than the lower one, so that when the falcon lifts her foot it may not be hurt by the pressure of the knot against it.

Shaping the jess around the leg

Some falconers widen the jess where it encircles the leg. This makes the jess somewhat clumsy and a well-mannered hawk should not require this. Goshawks, when not in flying order, might bate frequently and with great power, and it may be wise to widen jesses for such hawks. Whether snipping the edge of the jess makes much difference to the comfort of the hawk is difficult to judge, but it certainly does no harm. With all species of hawk I like to use jesses that are as thin and as short as possible, consistent with sufficient strength, so that the hawk is not too cluttered up with wide jesses, bewit, ring and transmitter. I prefer that the smooth side of the leather goes against the leg and I put the jess on so that the short end of the jess, point D, ends up on the outside of the leg. If, when jessing a hawk, you start off with point D to the outside, when you have finished the knot the point will still be on the outside of the leg.

As already stated, jesses should be cut from sound, well stretched leather. The leather should not tear easily; it is easy to test a jess before putting it on to a hawk by hooking your little finger through slit C and pulling as hard as you can. To help guard against tearing always punch a small hole at the 'working' ends of the slits. Keep the slits at A and B as small as possible, only just big enough to push the jess through; too long a slit can sometimes trap a beak tip or a claw. The slit at C should be only just big enough to slip over the swivel to be used. Jesses and leather leashes should be greased regularly. Kho-cho-line, a red dressing stocked by most saddlers, is excellent.

Length

Do not make your jesses extra long in the belief that it will give your hawk more freedom of movement. *Long jesses are dangerous.* When on the block there is a great danger of long jesses straddling the block (*see* chapter 2), trapping the hawk against the base of the block, invariably breaking her tail feathers and rarely improving her temper. On the screen perch a hawk with long jesses might well reach her neighbour; bating along the screen will break tail feathers and the hawk will find it more difficult to climb back up the screen. When a hawk is flying, long jesses are even more dangerous. They easily catch in bushes or wrap around wire fences. If flying a hawk with traditional jesses, always wet the ends and twist them so they have less chance to snag on anything after you have removed the leash and swivel.

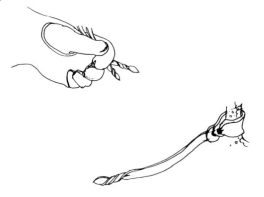

Fig. 39 Wet the ends of the jesses and twist them before flying a hawk

Although your hawk's jesses should be strong, it is important to see that your swivel and leash are yet stronger. At least then if your hawk should break away from her perch it will be the jesses that break the easiest and she will only get away with short pieces of broken jess rather than jesses, swivel or even part of her leash to handicap her.

Aylmeri jesses

Falconers have long searched for a way of reducing the risk of a hawk being caught up by her jesses. As early as 1857 Brodrick was using a shortened version of the traditional jess (*see* Brodrick painting reproduced in *O For a Falconer's Voice* by Roger Upton (The Crowood Press, 1987).

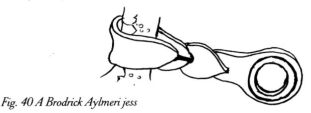

Fig. 40 A Brodrick Aylmeri jess

These jesses were put on in the same way as the traditional jess but were very short and ended in an eyelet. When on the block or screen an extension was slipped through the eyelet in the same way as is now used with Aylmeri jesses. The jesses, which were named after Major Guy Aylmer, are sometimes a little clumsy in appearance, particularly on small hawks, but they are very practical and safe.

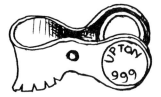

Fig. 41 Two methods of attaching Aylmeri jesses to legs

Above are two alternative ways of putting on Aylmeri. With the design on the left you have a spare flap on which you can fasten a name and address tag if you so wish. The pattern on the right is more suitable on small hawks. (*See* patterns and measurements at the end of this book.)

With any of the above patterns of eyelet jesses you will need a pair of button jesses to slip through the eyelets. Of course, with the Brodrick pattern you will need a rather shorter jess than with the Aylmeri patterns. For home use the jesses require a slit at C as normal, but when flying the hawk these can be exchanged for 'field jesses' in which there are no slits. 'Field jesses' are not normally needed with long wing hawks which can be flown with no false jesses in their Aylmeri. With sparrow-hawks it is possible to use pieces of string with a knotted button as 'field jesses'. Although they may be lost in the excitement of the flight, a spare supply can be carried in the pocket.

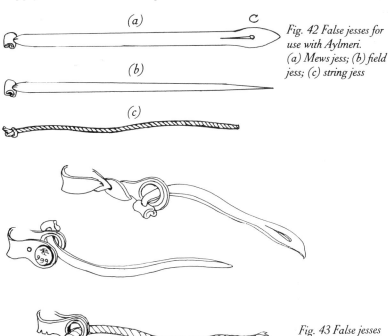

Fig. 42 False jesses for use with Aylmeri. (a) Mews jess; (b) field jess; (c) string jess

Fig. 43 False jesses attached to Aylmeri

Swivels

Swivels should be strong and they should swivel freely. It is best if they are of a shape that is easy to remove from and re-thread on to the jesses with one hand.

Fig. 44 Fitting a swivel to jesses

Various designs are advocated by their supporters as the best swivel, but for ease of use the old design, as shown below, top left, was ideal, However, these old swivels, made of soft brass with an iron pin that quickly rusted, were far from reliable. Swivels made to the same pattern but in modern materials would suit well. I still use the stainless steel, deep-sea fishing swivels originally made by Hardy's of Alnwick. They seem to last for ever and are perfect, but alas they are no longer produced.

Fig. 45 shows just a few of the many patterns of swivel in use today. The two designs on the right are at fault. With both patterns the jesses have a tendency to slip down on to the joint in the swivel and so restrict its freedom of movement. Most of the others are suitable provided they are made of stainless steel and are fairly rigid to handle. I find that the ball-bearing swivel (bottom row, middle of Fig. 45) with its floppy rings, made by Sampo Manufacturing Co., particularly difficult to use and impossible to get off in a hurry. Swivels should not be too large as this demands a large slit in the end of the jesses (this is a potential hazard), nor should they be too heavy. Heavy swivels swing like a pendulum as a hawk jumps back to its perch and can get tangled up with the leash and jesses. Fulco Tosti, a falconer of great experience, normally uses the ordinary iron swivels found on a dog lead. He argues that if strong enough for a dog it should hold a hawk.

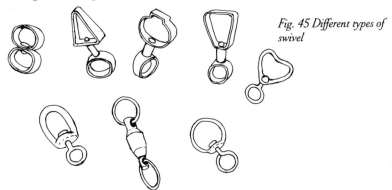

Fig. 45 Different types of swivel

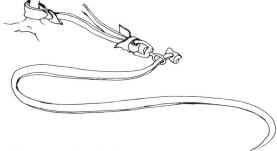

Fig. 46 Jesses, swivel and leash

Leashes

Leather leashes are still used by many falconers, but they have been replaced in a lot of cases by nylon webbing or log-line. Leather leashes made up from red buffalo rawhide (as are some steeplechase jockeys' stirrup leathers), chrome tanned cowhide (sometimes called 'porpoise hide'), or oiled Spanish cowhide are all very strong and long lasting. As with jesses, such leashes should be greased once a week. Many modern leashes are made up from nylon/Terylene log-line or webbing. Both serve the purpose very well and are extremely strong and reliable, provided that the knot or stop at the swivel end of the leash is really secure. When new, these leashes are rather slippery, so it is well worth rubbing a piece of beeswax or a candle along the length of the leash so that the knot used to tie them to the perch is more secure.

  With all leashes it is most important that the knot or button on the end of the leash is large enough so that it cannot possibly pull through the lower ring of the swivel. With nylon leashes I make a small loop in the end, rather than a simple knot, then fuse the knot so formed by heating it with a match. When a hawk is tied to the block I thread the end of the leash back through the loop and pull it up tight to the swivel before tying it to the perch. If the hawk bates, she pulls the knot tighter and the loop (which should only just be big enough to allow the end of the leash to be slipped through it) keeps the knot neatly up against the swivel.

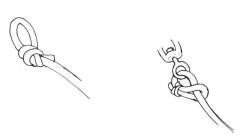

Fig. 47 An alternative to the 'button' at the end of a leash

Fig. 48 A knot and leather stop on a nylon/ terylene leash

Fig. 49 A half-hitch in a leash to stop it sliding through the swivel

If an ordinary knotted end is preferred (again, the knot should be fused together by heating) it is sound practice to slide a square of thick leather up against the knot to take some of the wear.

To guard against the leash sliding up through the swivel, some falconers loop the knot back around the shank of the leash to form a half-hitch.

With a flat webbing leash, a button can be formed at the end in the same way as with a leather leash. The free end of the webbing should be touched with a match to seal it and, after punching the hole through the button, it is a good idea to put a heated nail or screwdriver through the hole to fuse the ends of the fibres.

Fig. 50 A 'button' placed in the end of a leather or webbing leash

Fig. 51 An elastic 'shock absorber' in a leash

Tying the leash to a perch

For the larger hawks a leash should measure about 4ft 6in (1.45m) in length. When tying the leash to the block, ring or bow perch allow about 2ft–2ft 6in (62–77cm) in length, using the rest of the leash to tie at least two falconers' knots, with a half-hitch between them. It has been said that the greater the number of knots, the older and wiser the falconer. Some falconers seem to take delight in giving their hawks a great length of leash. Only a restless hawk will 'benefit' from the additional length and in doing so will jar its arms unnecessarily by gaining rather more speed when bating from the block. A well mannered hawk is little affected by the length of her leash. A shorter length of leash is also far less likely to get wound about the block. With hawks that are restless and bate strongly, as goshawks do on occasion on the lawn, it is possible to incorporate a shock absorber of catapult elastic into the leash. However, such additions might get tangled up with a leash or perch.

To tie a leash to the block, ring or bow perch, it is necessary to learn to tied the 'falconers' knot' with one hand.

Having tied the knot, slide it tightly up against the ring on the perch and thread the spare end of the leash through the loop of the knot. It is important to keep the hawk securely held on the fist until at least the first knot is tied. Do not hold her beside the perch for she will surely attempt to jump to it. Hold her directly above the perch.

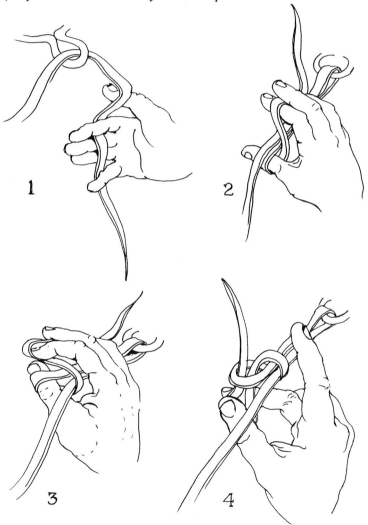

Fig. 52 The falconer's knot

Falconry furniture

Fig. 53 Two falconer's knots and a half-hitch

Fig. 54 A half-hitch is tied in the leash before it is secured to a 'screen' perch

When tying a hawk to the screen perch, first knot the leash at roughly half its length around the swivel ring.

With leather leashes it was once the practice to make a small slit in the leash about half-way down its length to thread the end of the leash through. This is inclined to weaken the leash and it is better to knot the leash as above or to wrap it again through the swivel.

Still holding the hawk on the glove, rest the glove on the top of the screen perch above the slit cut in the hessian screen. Throw one end of the leash over the perch, keeping the button end of the leash on the near side. Pull the long end of the leash through the slit in the screen, then, holding both ends of the leash in your spare hand, set the hawk down on to the perch. Tie a half bow and tuck the ends of the leash twice through the loop so formed. The ends can be tucked inside the slit in the hessian.

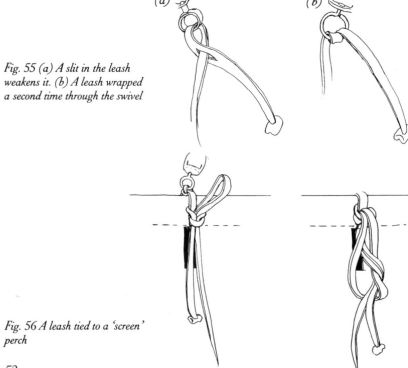

Fig. 55 (a) A slit in the leash weakens it. (b) A leash wrapped a second time through the swivel

Fig. 56 A leash tied to a 'screen' perch

Bells and bewits

In addition to jesses, the trained hawk in the West is furnished with bells. Bells are of great value in finding a temporarily lost hawk on her kill. They are also helpful in the hawking field when, for instance, a hawk is waiting-on. Instead of having to watch her all the time, the gay ringing of her bells will alert the falconer to her movements. Bells, normally a pair are used on each hawk, should be of different tone (Pakistani falconers call them 'nar u mada', male and female) to create a discordant jangle – a pleasing background sound to any falconer. Bells are available from the majority of hawk furniture suppliers. Pakistani bells are still available (though hardly up to the standard of pre-war supplies) and bells are custom-made in the USA, England and Germany on a commercial scale: such is the demand. Many falconers are skilled craftsmen who make hoods, gloves and even bells for their own use and as welcome gifts among friends.

Bells are attached to the legs, above the jesses, with small straps called bewits. No. 1 and no. 3 patterns are put on in exactly the same way as traditional jesses. No. 3 pattern has a short length of leather to C on to which can be attached a small name and telephone number plate. Pattern

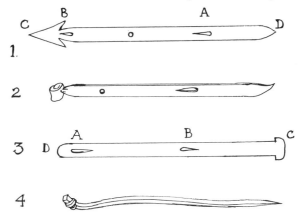

Fig. 57 Bewits. 1. Traditional bewit. 2. Button bewit. 3. Bewit with an extension for a name tag. 4. Pakistani bewit

Fig. 58 (a) A bell on a traditional bewit.
(b) A name tag

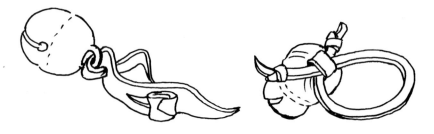

Fig. 59 A button bewit   *Fig. 60 A Pakistani bewit*

no. 2 is known as a button bewit. It is easily removed which is useful if a fellow falconer has lost his hawk and is confused or distracted by the sound of your bells.

Bewit no. 4 is very simple, but is effective. A strip of strong leather is knotted at one end. The bewit is then slipped through the loop on the bell, wrapped about the hawk's leg, and then again threaded through the loop on the bell. It is eased up until reasonably tight, then again knotted. Any spare leather can be snipped off.

A modern alternative to the leather bewit is a small-sized cable-tie which is available from electricians. These are effective and cheap, but do not look attractive and may be rather abrasive against the leg of the hawk.

Bells are not cheap and falconers are sometimes loathe to put them on to a new hawk for fear that she might bite at and damage them. It is better to use second-rate or old bells from the start so that the hawk will be accustomed to them; she will then be less likely to be bothered by them and will leave them alone. Later, when she is to fly, you can replace them with good bells. Likewise, in the non-flying season, by all means replace your best bells or take one of the pair off, but do keep a bell on her if she is not to be turned into a pen. The ringing of a bell might well deter a marauding cat or fox; at the least, it could alert somebody in the house to the impending danger.

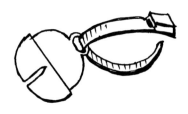

Fig. 61 A cable-tie bewit

Tail bells

Short winged hawks, goshawks or sparrowhawks are often belled on the tail rather than on the leg. They frequently rouse and shake their tail even when sitting fairly still and hidden in a tree or bush. Properly made tail bells have a different shank, but an ordinary large hawk bell will do as well.

Sketch no. 1 shows the traditional tail bewit cut from stiff leather. No. 2 shows how this is attached to the two centre (deck) feathers of the tail, close up to the body of the hawk. The ends are bound tightly with waxed thread or fine brass wire. The third drawing shows a modern alternative using elastoplast tape. This is threaded through the shank of the bell to half its length; then the tape is wound both up and down the quill of one of the deck feathers.

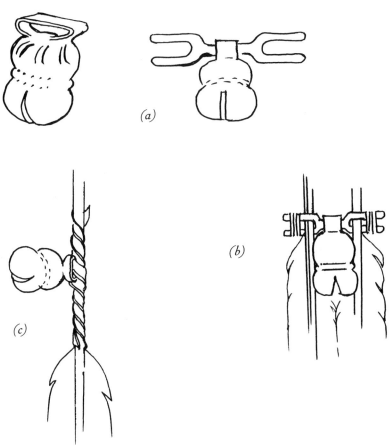

Fig. 62 (a) A tail bell and a bell with a tail bewit. (b) A bell attached to the tail feathers. (c) A bell attached to a single tail feather with elastoplast tape

Hoods

A well-fitting hood should meet certain criteria. Few meet them all. A hood should fit well and be comfortable to the hawk yet, with the braces tightened, it should be impossible to take it off. The beak opening should be such that it gives the best possible freedom for a hawk to feed or cast through the hood, but it should completely blindfold the hawk and should not let in light around the beak opening or through seams. The braces, when being opened or closed, should not catch or pinch any of the small feathers at the nape of the neck.

The hood should retain its shape, or be easily returned to its shape after rough treatment, such as being stuffed into an already crowded pocket. The leather should be dye-fast, that is the colour dye used on the leather should not run if the hood gets wet. The hood should not go limp or floppy, or stretch out of shape when wet. Either the hood or any trim on it should be of a bright colour so that it is easily found if dropped in the field.

Hoods used today come in a great variety of designs, but usually owe their origins to three main types.

The Arab hood

The Arab hood is basically a lightweight, sometimes quite soft, leather bag. It has a shaped beak opening and braces at the back which, when tightened, gather together the leather, like a drawstring on a pouch, rather than close an opening as in other hoods.

The Arab hood is comfortable for the hawk; the beak opening permits a hawk to cast without great difficulty and such hoods are rarely pulled off by a hawk, although some will indeed come off when braced up. The

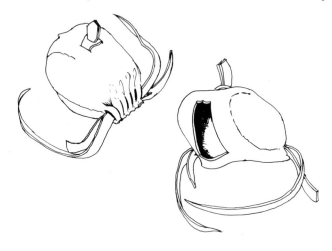

Fig. 63 Arab hoods

braces, threaded through slits in the back of the hood so as to concertina it when closed, do not catch feathers at the nape. If squashed flat, the hood can be immediately pushed back into shape. Being made from rather soft leather, Arab hoods are inclined to stretch and to let in light about the beak opening. They are made from a great variety of patterns and a shape that fits a saker very well may not suit a peregrine, even if reduced exactly to the proper size. The various patterns all fit into three types.

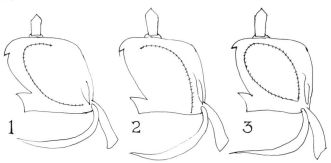

Fig. 64 Note the position of the seams on the three types of Arab hood

The commonest pattern, found throughout Arabia, is no. 1 above. Nos 2 and 3 come from Syria. As can be seen, the so-called Dutch or European hood closely follows no. 2 type in pattern and it is easy to see how the design was reputedly brought back by the returning Crusaders from Syria. Indeed, Emperor Frederick II claims to have introduced the hoods to Western Europe after he had seen them in use in the Middle East. No. 3 type is almost, if not quite, identical to the hood illustrated in Salvin and Brodrick's *Falconry in the British Isles* (1855), captioned 'taken from a Syrian pattern.'

The Dutch hood

The Dutch hood proper, produced in large numbers until the early part of this century by the professional falconers at Valkenswaard in Holland, was little altered from those used in earlier times in Europe and Britian, as can be seen by those few early hoods that grace our museums.

The hood is made up from three pieces of quite stiff and thick leather. If correctly made to the pattern, the Dutch hood is comfortable but heavy. The beak opening does not allow the hawk to cast, and the braces are likely to catch feathers at the nape. Because it is hard and moulded in shape, it will stand up to quite rough handling, but if squashed it requires re-moulding and is not easily used until that is done. In fact, it would seem that since being brought from the Middle East the design has lost many of its advantages and can hardly be regarded as an improvement on its ancestor.

Passage peregrine with Dutch hood proper

The Dutch hood was traditionally trimmed with green or red baize on the side panels and this, being pulled into the seam as the hoods were stitched, made the joints completely light proof. Some of the later hoods from Valkenswaard, made by Karl Mollen, did not incorporate these cloth panels and often leaked light, easily seen by holding the hood up against the light. The Dutch hood was also gaily attired with a feather and wool plume, bound with brass wire. Today there are many hood makers producing beautifully crafted and ornate Dutch style hoods or Syrio-Dutch hoods as the variant based on the Salvin and Brodrick Syrian hood is usually called.

Fig. 65 The Dutch hood

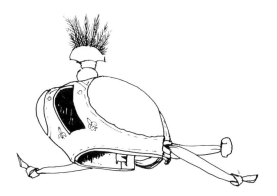

Fig. 66 The Syrio-Dutch hood

Many of these modern hoods are an improvement on the old Valkenswaard hood, being lighter in weight – a return to the original Syrian hood. However, they are often spoilt by falconers attempting to improve the beak opening to the shape used in the Indian hood. I find that with a Dutch pattern this allows the hood to sit back too close to the eyes of the hawk, but perhaps I have just been unlucky in the hoods I have tried out. Other modern hood makers have gone the other way and have produced an Arab pattern hood of very stiff leather. Some also try to incorporate an Indian-style beak opening. Both points are doubtful improvements on the original design.

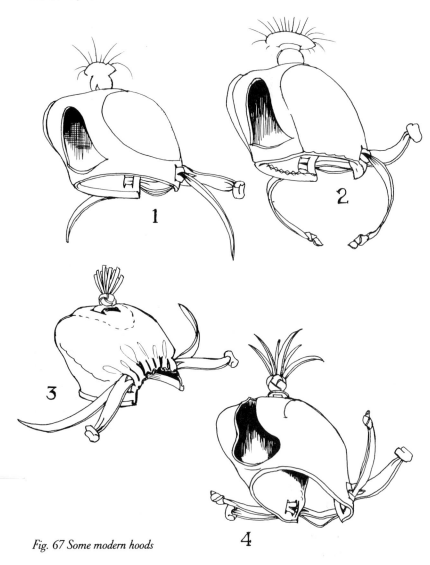

Fig. 67 Some modern hoods

Of the above designs I find no. 1 and no. 4 fit quite well, although no. 4 is a tall hood and pressures the top of the crop. No. 2, with its wide beak opening, allows the hood to sit back on to the eyes, which is clearly illustrated when the hood is taken off after only a short period by the damp patches inside. No. 3 has lost all of the advantages of the Arab hood; it is made of thick leather, the beak opening is too wide at the base and the back of the hood doesn't round over far enough, thereby tightening against the back of the skull rather than curving neatly under the bone.

 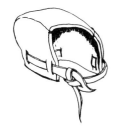

Fig. 68 Dutch rufter hoods

Dutch rufter hoods are rarely made or used today. The Dutch falconers used rufter hoods on hawks when first trapped. The hood had no plume or cloth panels which meant that the hawk had nothing that a scratching claw could hook into and so possibly pull off. The neck size could be adjusted to a nicety; this is not always possible with the hood proper.

The Anglo-Indian hood

The third type of hood commonly used today is that styled the Anglo-Indian hood. This has been adapted from the original Indian hood.

The Indian hood does not open or close at the back, being sewn up the back seam. It is tapped into place on the the hawk's head. As the hood cannot be opened or closed, it is possible for a hawk to pull it off. However, the Indian falconers maintain that provided the hood fits well, and that the hawk is properly broken to the hood and does not get it off in the first few days, she will happily sit for many hours without attempting to scratch it off.

*Immature captive bred peregrine falcon
with a perfectly-fitting Anglo-Indian hood*

Fig. 69 The Indian hood

English falconers soon realised the advantages of these hoods, particularly that they were barely half the weight of a Dutch hood. By cutting open the back seam and inserting Dutch style braces they hopefully combined the best of both hoods, and so was born the Anglo-Indian hood. They are comfortable for the hawk, being well bossed out over the eyes; they are light in weight, yet do not easily lose their shape however treated; and they have a nicely shaped beak opening, giving a hawk complete freedom to feed or cast. Provided they are cut out to a good pattern, they do stay on well and are not easily pulled off when the braces are closed. Some hawks do not like the somewhat tight throatlatch, and being of lightweight leather they are liable to stretch, losing their shape and letting light in around the beak opening. The hoods are easy and cheap to make.

One problem often encountered with Anglo-Indian hoods is feathers getting caught up in the braces as they are opened. Normally, if the falconer rebraces the hood, then again strikes the braces, the feathers will clear. Various methods have been tried to help overcome this problem. The whole of the back opening can be filled in with a triangular piece of soft leather (wash leather is ideal) or the working part of the braces can be covered with an extending fold of leather. Some falconers fold the extension to the outside of the hood, others to the inside.

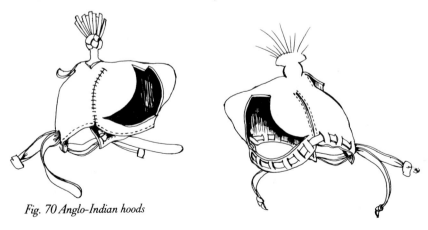

Fig. 70 Anglo-Indian hoods

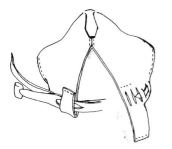

Fig. 71 An extension to the hood to cover the braces

Of course, the Anglo-Indian hood or indeed the Arab hood can be decorated with a wool and feather plume, as is normal on a Dutch hood. However, a neat leather tag or Turk's head knot, which can be made up in bright coloured leathers, is more practical and long-lasting in the field.

One drawback with all hoods is their tendency to become soft and to lose shape when wet. I treat my hoods with Kho-cho-line, which proofs them to a degree. A silicone spray or Barbour coat dressing might prove better. One friend used to shine his hoods with shoe polish; some hood makers varnish their hoods. However well you might proof the hood, braces get wet and jam tight. It is then that many falconers discover for the first time that their expensive and grand hood will come off even when braced up! If near home, the best remedy is a hair dryer.

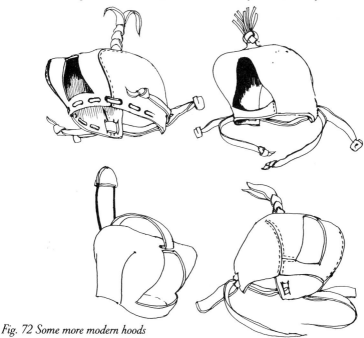

Fig. 72 Some more modern hoods

Braces

Braces need to be made of strong leather, but they should also be flexible enough to thread easily through the slits in the back of the hood. Some falconers prefer stiff braces that stand out well from the hood. The braces on the old Dutch hoods were like this but were always too short, making it difficult to get hold of them with teeth and fingers (when a hawk is on your fist you have to undo the braces with your teeth and spare hand). Pigskin or modelling calf is suitable for making stiff braces.

Other falconers prefer floppy braces and these are certainly better for being reasonably long, although not so long that they are continually getting under the hawk's feet or muddled up with her food. Although it might be thought that soft braces dangling about her shoulders would annoy a hawk, in practice they don't seem to bother her at all. Most Arab falconers use soft braces on their hoods and many of their hawks are fine examples of content, well-manned hawks properly trained to the hood.

Traditionally, and conveniently, the opening braces are usually buttoned at the end (as the button on the end of a leash) and the closing braces are either knotted or left free. This is helpful in ensuring that the correct braces are pulled. The opening braces are also shorter in length. However, some hawks get very clever at catching hold of a brace button, and snare it between claw and toe. If they succeed in loosening the braces or dragging the hood off, it will soon become a confirmed habit. They invariably do this on the same side of the hood as before. If the button is cut off, the brace will then hopefully slip through between toe and claw as the hawk pulls. Arab hoods are usually made with no buttons or knots on the brace ends and they are perfectly practical in use. For the same reason it is better not to decorate the hood with anything in which a hawk may easily hook a claw.

Braces often are too tight either to open or to close easily; more frequently they are too loose to keep the hood closed. Tight braces will usually work better after some use, or the slits in the back of the hood can be eased a little by inserting a small screw-driver or awl and very carefully enlarging the holes a fraction.

To help prolong the useful life of a pair of braces various methods can be used to make them grip more tightly again. An additional tab of leather can be slipped through the brace slits at the back of the hood. A small cable tie can be fastened (not too tightly) around both braces either side of where they run through the slits, or an elastic band can be used in the same way. The braces can be taken out and replaced on opposite sides. Alternatively, one brace can be removed, turned over and replaced with flesh-side of the leather to flesh-side, that is sueded side to sueded side. For a 'temporary' repair, wet or 'suck' the braces where they overlap in the middle before putting the hood on the hawk and doing it up.

Storage of hoods

When not in use Arab hoods are better stored with the braces closed. This keeps the back gathers neatly folded. All other types of hood should be stored with the braces opened. If kept in this way, the hood settles to its open shape, so making it easy to put on to a hawk. Of course, when pulled close the braces will shut the hood properly. If, however, the hood is kept with the braces closed, when it is opened it will have a tendency to stay closed, or partly so, making it difficult to use and unpleasant for the hawk. For the same reason it is important that Dutch type hoods should be cut from the correct patterns so that they will stand open at the back.

Always keep hoods clean, particularly inside: it is surprising how often there is a small piece of dried meat stuck inside the beak opening. Arab falconers blow into a hood before using it so that there is no dust or sand to get into the eyes of the hawk. In hot countries it might be of value to punch a couple of small holes into the top of the hood, near to the plume. As their heads get hot, hawks are more inclined to scratch at the hood. Check that the braces are not caught up inside. If the hood is trimmed with a plain leather tag, I find it more comfortable in use if the tag is sideways-on rather than facing the front of the hood.

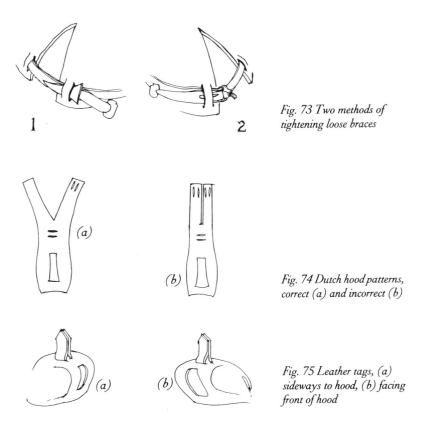

Fig. 73 Two methods of tightening loose braces

Fig. 74 Dutch hood patterns, correct (a) and incorrect (b)

Fig. 75 Leather tags, (a) sideways to hood, (b) facing front of hood

Hawking bags

Hawking bags are useful for carrying the lure, spare hood, creance and any quarry the hawks might have taken. The Mollens at Valkenswaard made hawking bags until well into this century which were virtually the same as those used for the previous two or three hundred years – if one is to judge from early paintings and tapestries.

Fig. 76 Mollen hawking bag

These bags were hung from a swivel which allowed easy access to both sides. They were made up in green baize, cut out by the Mollen family but stitched together by the local tailor, Mr Gevers. Hung from a broad leather belt, the bag was usually slung from the left shoulder. When a falconer was riding, it was often hung from a waist belt. In those days a bag cost £2.10s.0d. Today many hawk furniture suppliers make up a variety of bags, from traditional patterns to simple modern variations on the same theme, hanging from a swivel.

Equally suitable for use as a hawking bag are many of the game fishing bags on the market. Barbour catalogue an ideal bag, called 'The Tarras', in two sizes. These bags have a washable and removable lining and two small pockets on the front which are just right for housing the hood, leash and swivel. If you must use an ornate hood, then place an open-topped can in one of the pockets into which you can drop your hood.

Other old pictures show falconers with their lure slung over their shoulder, which doesn't seem very practical as it would be on full view to any hawk on the wing or unhooded.

Hawking jacket

A bag is certainly not necessary when flying a sparrowhawk or merlin. Everything that is needed in the field is small enough to be carried in pockets. Of recent years I have found it more convenient and comfortable to use a custom-made jacket, with an abundance of pockets (two particularly large ones for lure and quarry), when hawking on the grouse moors. A skeet jacket or shooting waistcoat, with large cartridge pockets, would serve equally well and these are available off the peg from most gun shops.

If out with a large team of hawks, when one might reasonably expect to take four or five brace of grouse, a member of the party furnished with an ordinary game bag will hopefully carry most of the quarry.

Carrying hoods when hawking

Although it is a mistake to put a hood in the same pocket as the lure, quarry, penknife, etc., I have found that an Anglo-Indian or an Arab type hood comes to little harm if put in a separate small pocket. Many falconers are nothing if not ingenious and I have seen hoods hung on dog clips sewn to hawking bag or jacket; large napkin safety pins clipped through lapel and hood throatlash; and a neat little strap and buckle with which the hood was safely anchored to the bag strap. The drawbacks to all of these methods is that the hoods get pulled out of shape, become wet if the weather is unkind, and continually get caught up with the lure line or telemetry cable.

Some falconers even go to the length of carving a hawk-head shaped block which they screw to their belt. The hood is slipped over the block and braced up. Presumably if such a falconer were flying two or three different hawks, for instance a peregrine falcon and tiercel and a gyrfalcon he would require three separate blocks screwed to his belt! Although a block would keep the hood in shape, the plume on the hood would be knocked with every movement of the arm, and with two blocks you could play 'cats' cradles' with your lure line! Undoubtedly any type of hood is better off out of the way in a pocket, if necessary protected by an open-topped tin can as suggested above.

A knife may prove useful at times. Nothing is better than a clasp knife of good make, with a locking blade. Choose one with a loop at one end, then tie it with a length of cord to your hawking bag or button hole. As you take off the leash and swivel when preparing to fly your hawk, immediately put your swivel back on to the leash (also, your false jesses if using Aylmeri, and, as with the hood, put them deep in a pocket in a coat or hawking bag).

Lures

The simplest lure is a dead grouse, rook or rabbit, according to what quarry you wish to fly with your hawk. However, for convenience a made-up lure is necessary and useful whether you are flying long or short winged hawks.

Lures have traditionally been constructed on a wood or horseshoe base that is well wrapped in tow and covered in leather or felt. A swivel is securely attached at the top of the lure to which a line or strap can be tied. Although too heavy for general use, these lures are handy in early training, helping to ensure that a hawk does not learn to carry the lure or quarry away at the approach of the falconer. Some hawks will attempt to drag a lure to shade, to hide under a bush or to the edge of a field, not necessarily trying to get away from the falconer. They are more prone to do this if being called to the lure near other hawks.

Provided a hawk gets the reward of meat when she comes to the lure, it is immaterial what the lure looks like. She can be trained to a lure made up from a soup plate or a flat cap. However, it is normal practice to garnish a lure with the dried wings of the potential quarry, or, for a goshawk, with the skin of a rabbit.

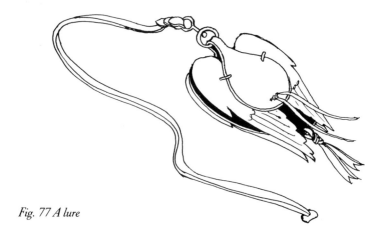

Fig. 77 A lure

Preparation and care of lures

To prepare wings for use as a lure, cut them from the pelt at the second wing joint, the elbow, and put the wings in the plate-warming oven in the kitchen (the cool oven on a four door Aga is ideal for the purpose). If you don't want to upset the cook, put them on a few layers of newspaper and leave them for some days. If you do use cured wings on your lure it is better to partly cover them with leather so that meat can be tied to the lure without coming into contact with the wings.

Mallard wings seem to stand up to wear and tear particularly well and will suit a game hawk, as will grouse or pheasant wings. A rook hawk is better trained to a lure with rook or crow wings. Certainly, the use of a black lure is often sufficient encouragement to a hawk to 'have a go' at the real thing. A heavy lure is not very convenient to carry in the field and so once the hawk can be trusted not to carry the lure a much lighter one of the same pattern can be used.

If a falconer intends to stoop his hawk at the lure it is even more important that he uses a well-padded lure of just sufficient weight, when garnished, to swing at the end of the line. With a lightweight lure it is better to use a long lure line wound around a length of dowelling that has been sharpened at one end. If the hawk is at all nervous the lure can be pegged down by pushing the stick into the ground.

When swinging the lure the correct length of line can be fixed by half-hitching the line a couple of times around the stick. I now use a very small lure of medium weight. The lure is not trimmed with cured wings but is garnished with fresh grouse wings each day. I use a leather lure line, about 4ft 6in to 5ft (1.45 to 1.60m) in length, with a leash button at the hand end so it is easily held without slipping through the fingers.

When lures were carried slung over the shoulder and hanging on the falconer's right-hand side, the lure leash had a button at one end and a slit at the other through which the button could be slipped to hold the lure in place. When in use the button was allowed to slide up against the swivel on the lure and the falconer could slip a finger or two through the slit in the other end of the line to hold it securely.

One of the simplest, easy to clean lures, which is used by a well respected falconer, consists of the folded layers of a discarded lorry inner tube. This type of lure is held together by nylon strings which are threaded right through it and which may be used to tie meat to it. Some falconers tie on a few streamers of red tape to the tail of the lure. However, any meat tied to a lure should be securely fastened; nothing is more likely to teach hawks bad manners than if they can manage to pull the food from the lure and fly off with it.

Natural lures

A lazy man's lure, yet certainly one of the most effective, is the dead quarry at which the hawk is normally flown. Many grouse falconers take out from the previous day's bag a big, tough old grouse that will stand a certain amount of being thrown out on the heather. One friend has even recommended this as a method of tenderising a tough old cock sufficiently for it to be of use in the kitchen!

It may be necessary to attach a line to the dead bird, particularly if it is small and as easily carried as a grey partridge, or if you are flying a large falcon with a tendency to carry. Tie the line to both wings, not to the legs of the pelt; a clove hitch is ideal for this purpose. It is surprising how easily a falcon can lift even an old cock grouse, particularly from a

Fig. 78 Line for a 'natural' lure

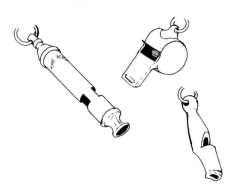

Fig. 79 Different types of whistle

hillside in a strong wind. Nothing is more embarrassing than to see your hawk carry off a thrown out grouse even though it does happen from time to time.

Hawking whistles

Hawks will learn quickly to associate a particular sound with feeding, returning to the lure or the imminent flush of quarry. Some falconers train their hawks to respond to a whistle and an 'Acme Thunderer' or referee's whistle is ideal. However, when game hawking it is important that the hawk whistle should not confuse the dogs that are working for you, nor indeed should the dog whistle confuse the hawk. If you use a staghorn or buffalo horn pealess whistle for the dogs, then no confusion should arise. Some dog handlers use the powerful Thunderer whistle as a back up to the ordinary one. One friend has knicknamed his Acme Thunderer 'The Last Resort'.

It is possible that one could use the same whistle to call up the hawk as to make the dog drop or sit. However, I find one whistle quite enough to manage, and so rely on a shout to attract the attention of my hawk. Shouting can become very noisy but some falconers would never seem the same, nor indeed get the same successful results, without their loud but highly individual ways of encouraging their hawks to return and mount over the ever patient dogs.

The creance

The creance is a long, light but strong line used when training the hawk. These days braided nylon suits the purpose very well. A length of 100yd (90m) is more than enough and is best kept wound on to a stick or on an old fishing reel. If you do keep it wound round a stick, remember to drill a tiny hole through the stick. Thread the end of the line through this hole and knot it tightly. When in use the creance should never be tied to the swivel but to both jesses, and enough line should be run out so that the hawk only feels the restraint of the creance if she overshoots the fist or lure. The line should never ever be allowed to trail behind the hawk without a weight or anchor on the end.

Transporting hawks

The field cadge

The field cadge is not seen often today, except on the grouse moors. It is a convenient way of transporting a team of hawks when on foot, and if in the care of a considerate cadger it is a good deal more comfortable for the hawks than being carried on the fist, possibly by an inexperienced member of the field. The surface of the cadge should not be as wide as a screen perch. The hawk sometimes needs to grip on to the cadge firmly to retain her balance, and this is easier if she can wrap her foot about the perch. Old wool carpeting makes an ideal surface but modern man-made fibre carpets are not suitable because the claws of the hawk snag in the pile. A canvas or leather surface is too slippery and is no help to the hawk in retaining her position.

A hawk should be tied to the cadge in the same way as she would be tied to the screen perch. It is important to remember to tuck the ends of the leash back through the loop of the knot. If this isn't done there is some danger that the cadger will step on the end of the leash as he picks up the cadge, thus untying a hawk. Some falconers use clips from a dog lead on the cadge, on to which they then clip the slits in the ends of the jesses. These falconers will find to their cost that it is easy for the hawk to get free, since the jesses slip from the clip as the hawk turns around and around. Adjustable shoulder straps make it much easier to keep the cadge steady in a wind and it also spreads the weight between hands and shoulders. With shoulder straps one hand is freed to untie or tie up the hawk and to lift a bating hawk back on to the cadge.

The legs of the cadge can be made to fold away but this is of no great advantage when the cadge is in use, only when equipment is being transported to the hill. The legs should be long enough to keep the tails of the hawks clear of the ground. However, if they are too long they are inclined to catch on long heather or scrub while the cadge is being carried, and make it more difficult to tuck the cadge down in a sheltered hollow on a windy day.

Falconry furniture

 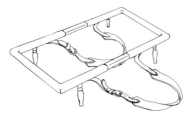

Fig. 80 A cadge, showing the 'brolly' and the pouch for spare hoods etc.

Fig. 81 A cadge, showing the shoulder straps

A cadge on the moor

On my cadge I have a small leather pouch tacked on one corner which contains a spare swivel and leash as well as a couple of spare hoods. It is surprising how often these have come in very handy. I also have a large gig brolly, or fishing or golfing umbrella, slung along one side of the cadge. This has been the cause of the occasional unkind comment about being 'afraid of a bit of rain', but many falconers and friends have been more than glad to test its covering capacity in a sudden rain storm. In light rain the cadger can keep himself and the spare hawks dry. It wasn't until I had lost one or two black umbrellas among the peat hags on the moor that I realized the value of the brightly coloured golf umbrellas now available in the shops.

A convenient size for a cadge is about 4ft (1.20m) by 1ft 10in (55cm). A very large cadge is both heavy and awkward to carry. One cadge, used for some years by friends, was made of aluminium, rounded at the ends, with legs that could be screwed out for transporting. Two European friends use a cadge made up from plastic plumber's piping as used in drains for sinks. This is light to carry and cheap to replace. The cadger wears a single carrying strap around his neck and this is attached to the frame of the cadge by the two front legs.

The pole cadge

This is an alternative that can be used to transport three or four hawks in the field. Such cadges have been used for merlins by no less an authority than E. B. Michell, author of *The Art and Practice of Hawking*, which was published in 1900. However, I find them both awkward to carry and easily caught and buffeted by any wind.

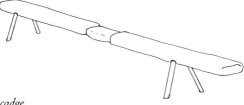

Fig. 82 A pole cadge

The box cadge

Box cadges are useful for transporting hawks and can be made up into almost any shape which is convenient to fit in the back of a car. This type of cadge should be of sufficient height to keep the tail tips well clear of mutes, and so designed that it will not easily tip over.

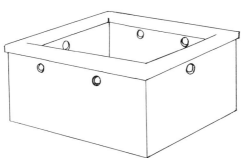

Fig. 83 A box cadge

Cars

Most hawks travel well in cars but do not care for hump back bridges or other road conditions where the perch suddenly sinks under them. A well mannered hawk will travel better unhooded if on a high perch. Echart Schormair has devised a very neat perch for his two well mannered peregrines that slots into the head-rest holes on the top of the passenger seat in his Toyota Land Cruiser.

 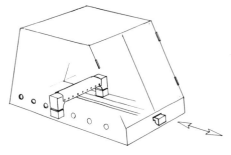

Fig. 84 A car head-rest perch   *Fig. 85 A travelling box with a sliding perch*

Travelling boxes

Some falconers find it more convenient to carry short-winged hawks in a travelling box. Again, great ingenuity has produced masterpieces of design, incorporating special air vents or sliding perches. As long as they are sufficiently roomy and the air holes are positioned as low as possible, the basic design can be adapted to please the maker. However, be careful when using a travelling box that the air holes are not covered by other luggage.

One sad story about travelling boxes concerns a falconer arriving in Scotland after the long, exhausting journey from the South. Although tired he was pleased with how well his goshawk had travelled in his newly constructed box. As he said, 'After the first part of the journey she settled down and I've had no movement from her at all.' Indeed, on opening the box the goshawk was found to be dead!

While serving in the Army in London I used to transport my merlins in a neat little box that could be carried like a suitcase; out of sight of inquisitive fellow travellers, this was a far better way of transporting them than an open box cadge.

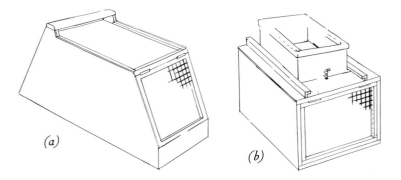

(a)

(b)

Fig. 86 Dog boxes: (a) with a perch at one end; (b) to fit in a Land Rover with a box cadge to slide in on top

Perches can be built in to cross-country vehicles, for example, for easy access when rook hawking. Alternatively, it is sometimes convenient to incorporate the hawk perches into the design of a dog box such as you may use for your pointers or setters when game hawking. Some falconers make ingenious provision for the box cadge or field cadge to slide or clip into the top of the dog box. While I find that hawks travel better parallel to the length of the car, other falconers are equally convinced that they are better sat across the vehicle.

When constructing boxes and perches do ensure that there is sufficient headroom for a hooded hawk, and that your beautifully designed and constructed boxes are not so exactly fitted that you cannot get them into or out of the vehicle.

Air travel

For air travel there is nothing better than a stout cardboard box. Plenty of airholes should be cut all around the box 2 or 3in (5 or 8cm) above the floor, and a square of carpet should be glued to the bottom of the box. Full IATA (International Air Transport Association) regulations contain the following notes.

Materials: fabric, fibreboard and wood.
Principles of design.
1. A strong corrugated fibreboard container with overlapping flaps. A series of ventilation holes shall be pierced around the lower half on all sides of the container about 3in (7.5cm) apart as well as two holes on all four sides near the top. These lower holes shall be of a diameter sufficient to allow light to filter through to permit the bird to see the food on the floor of the container.
2. A perch consisting of a block of wood of sufficient size to allow the bird a firm grip may be firmly fixed to the floor of the container, if desired. The birds can travel safely standing on their feet.
3. An inlet of approximately 3in (7.5cm) diameter should be provided at the top of the container for inserting the food. A fabric funnel which can be tied will provide an efficient closure if sewn to the box.
4. The container shall be large enough to carry one bird and to permit it to turn without stretching its wings to the fullest extent.

Fig. 87 An IATA 'Q' style box for transporting hawks by air

Further comments on travelling

It is important that the lining of the sides and the lid of the box should be absolutely smooth and slippery, made of material such as card or hardboard, so that the hawk cannot cling to it and so that open wings do not catch on it. It is better not to have a block of wood as a perch and hawks travel very well on a surface such as carpet which they can grip.

It is debatable whether a supply of food is necessary. Livestock should be given priority on air flights and, for all but the smallest of hawks, a journey of 24 to 48 hours without food is no hardship. Of course a hawk should not be shipped unless in good health and condition. Dropping food, which may well be far from fresh, into a box which has mutes and mess in the bottom, is of questionable value.

Fortunately, the average flight is of short duration, and it is easy to check beforehand to see if your flight is on time or is cancelled. In my experience the greatest hold-up occurs at the destination airport. I would prefer to box a hawk with a hood on, at least on the shorter journeys where feeding might not be necessary, taking care not to give the hawk casting with her last feed before her journey. The hawk's swivel and leash should be removed and her tail bound up with brown sticky paper. This should be done with the type of tape that you have to lick before using as this is easy to soak off with hot water.

Do not open the box until you are in a small room with the curtains drawn in case the hawk manages to get her hood off and flies from the box before you have got hold of the jesses. Only fools say that this could never happen to them.

Weighing the hawk

Scales on which the falconer can weigh his hawk, are an additional help in the constant balancing act of feeding the hawk the correct amount of food in relation to the amount of work she is doing, and thus getting maximum performance with just that degree of obedience necessary in the field. However, scales should not be regarded as the only means by

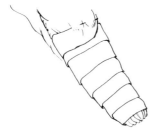

Fig. 88 A tail wrapped in brown paper for travelling

Fig. 89 Weighing scales with a perch

which the condition of a hawk is to be judged, even though the modern digital scales which are now available are probably rather more accurate than the old spring scales. It is, of course, necessary to adapt the top of the scales to accommodate a perch or platform on which the hawk can stand, and this should be positioned so that the wings and tail of the hawk are clear both of the scales and the table on which it stands.

Some falconers remove the swivel and the leash before weighing their hawk, thus sitting her unsecured on the scales. Whether hooded or unhooded it is silly ro risk a hawk damaging herself by flying off and hitting a wall or, worse, going through a glass window. It is a naïve falconer who believes his hooded hawk is safe untied. Provided that the hawk is weighed with the same furniture, and that the leash is held in the same way, there should be little variance in accuracy.

Weight, of course, is not the only factor which determines whether a hawk will work well, or indeed behave, in the field on a particular day. The weather conditions, the time of day that the hawk is flown, the amount of flying she had the previous day and the experience she has of the quarry are all factors which influence her performance. There is no doubt, however, that weighing can be a useful warning system, letting the falconer know when the hawk is up in weight or, even more important, low in condition.

Location-finding telemetry

One of the few modern inventions that has proved to be of help to the falconer is directional telemetry, which is used to locate a lost hawk. A transmitter – which emits the pulse signal – can be attached to either the leg or the tail of the hawk.

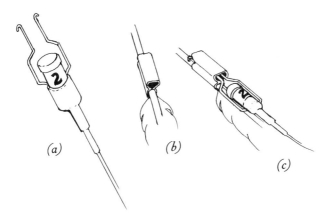

(a)   (b)   (c)

Fig. 90 (a) A transmitter for tail mounting. (b) A tail tube glued in to position. (c) A transmitter slotted into the tube

Tail mounting

For tail mounting the commonest method is to glue a small metal tube to one of the two deck feathers in the centre of the tail. This tube, which is permanent, should be placed as high up as possible near to the body of the hawk, without the risk of gluing it to the skin. When in the field, the transmitter is fitted with its batteries, checked to see that its signal comes through on the receiver and then slipped into position simply by pinching the two spring clips together and sliding them into the metal tube mounted on the hawk. Some manufacturers reverse the prongs so that the transmitter is carried even higher and there is less of the wire aerial trailing beyond the end of the tail.

Another method is to wrap a piece of leather around the shaft of the deck feather and then glue it firmly in place so that it stands out at right angles to the tail. The leather should be shaped as shown in fig. 92, with a small hole punched through it. The hole may then have an eyelet fitted into it as with an Aylmeri jess. The radio is attached with a length of freezer bag tie.

Yet another method of tail mounting does not require any permanent fixture on the tail of the hawk. A special 'T' mount on the transmitter slots into a double-jawed bulldog clip. This clip then fits on to both deck feathers.

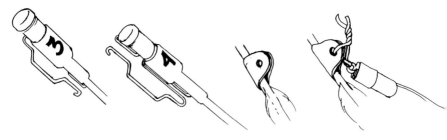

Fig. 91 Different positions for the spring prongs

Fig. 92 Leather tail-mount glued to a 'deck' feather

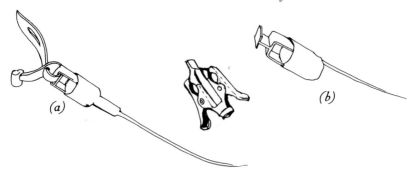

Fig. 93 (a) Leather bewit for the leg mounting of a transmitter. (b) Special transmitter T fitting with double Bulldog clip for tail mounting

Leg mounting

For attachment to the leg the transmitter is fitted with a button bewit. This can be buttoned either directly around the leg or, better still if you already have one, through the bell bewit. Instead of a proper leather bewit, a cable tie can be used. As ties cannot be undone it is necessary to cut them off at the end of the day and use a fresh cable tie each day.

The tail mount has certain advantages over the leg mount. Firstly, the transmitter is less likely to be knocked against the quarry or any perch on which the hawk might take stand. Secondly, being off the ground when the hawk has killed, the transmitter is also less likely to get wet, and this slight additional elevation can increase the distance at which the signal can be picked up by the receiver. Finally, the hawk is less likely to short across two electricity wires than with a leg mount.

Tiercel ready on the fist with a radio transmitter attached to his leg

However, there is a limit to how much a transmitter will stand being bitten and pulled at, and the deck feathers will not take kindly to constant attack. A famous old tiercel of my acquaintance has, on three or four occasions, neatly plucked out his own deck feather, tube and transmitter. It is probably worth while to put tail tubes on to your hawks early in their training and to accustom them to transmitters by clipping on dummy transmitters.

Some falconers even put two transmitters on to a hawk. On one occasion two of us were looking for the same hawk which we were sure had killed as he had not returned looking for us and the pointer. The hawk was fitted with two transmitters so we each tuned our receivers to a different transmitter. After searching for some distance we discovered that we were both getting good signals but in almost opposite directions. We each followed our own line; I found the jerkin on his grouse, my friend found the other transmitter, which had been knocked or pulled off. There will certainly be many improvements in the efficiency and range of such transmitters in the future, and I look forward to the day when we do not have the long, trailing aerial.

Unfortunately, many would-be falconers, and sadly some with rather more experience, seem to think that telemetry is the answer to many of the falconer's problems. They believe that the falconer does not have to bother any longer to fly his game hawk in open country when he can find her on her kill in the thickest cover with his receiver. However, this is not the case if the falconer still wants to experience proper waiting-on flights. A high waiting-on hawk still needs enough open space to come down from a high pitch at her rapidly moving quarry. If the partridge or grouse continually beat her to cover, she will soon lower her pitch. Fly a rook hawk in enclosed country and you may catch many rooks or crows in magpie-like rat-hunts, but you will rarely, if ever, get a high, ringing flight.

An even worse abuse of telemetry and the whole sport of falconry is when the falconer lets a hawk off self-hunting, hoping to find her with the receiver. Ah! she has killed a rook! What excellent rook hawking!

3

Eyasses, passagers, hacking and thoughts on training

Eyas hawks can either come from the wild, where at the present time they are extremely plentiful, or from captive bred stock. The wild population can clearly stand the minute demands of genuine falconers without any threat to their numbers, the only exception being the merlin which is at present under some pressure from loss of habitat. So far no distinction can be drawn between wild taken or captive bred eyasses. However, it is possible, given further generations of captive breeding, that offspring from proven parents (hawks that have shown their ability in the hawking field) will differ from those produced by commercial hawk farms. Already falconers are talking of certain captive bred families being good game hawks, natural at 'waiting-on', or being easy to train and quick to learn. It may be that in the future wise falconers will only bother to get fresh hawks from breeders who use their breeding stock for falconry in the field, because that is the only place where the abilities of the hawk can be tested.

Peregrines at hack

The pros and cons of hacking

The question of whether or not to hack the eyasses has long been the source of discussion among falconers. Hack is normally advised only for long winged hawks, peregrines, gyrs, sakers and so on, although sparrowhawks have been hacked to their advantage. The idea of hack is to give young hawks complete freedom to fly and to gain in strength and skill. The hawks return to the hack site for the food which is provided for them and this continues for a period of two to six weeks until the hawks start hunting in earnest.

The success enjoyed by many of the celebrated falconers of the past with hacked peregrines would suggest that they believed in the value of hack, as do many falconers today. Unhacked eyasses may have one or two points in their favour but on the whole the value of hack well outweighs any disadvantages. The unhacked hawk can begin its training as soon as it is 'hard penned', and its flight and tail feathers have grown to their full length. However, although they have a few weeks' advantage in beginning their training the unhacked hawks will often take longer in learning to fly adroitly at the lure. There is usually little advantage in being ready to fly too early in the year. For instance, the earliest a young peregrine can be flown at game is 12 August, and with all but the longest hack there is plenty of time to get the hawk ready by that date.

Eyasses ready to go out to hack

Unhacked hawks are not easily disappointed by early failures at quarry and will invariably try, try and try again. However, a hawk at hack may already have made many abortive attempts to catch passing pigeons or rooks and so may have some doubts about her ability to catch quarry. The unhacked hawk may well be expected to fail through clumsiness and lack of skill when first flown at quarry until repeated failure teaches her something. In contrast, the hacked hawk has every chance of success on her first or second essay at quarry with the help of falconer and dog. Thus what the hacked hawk learns by daily flying the unhacked hawk has to learn after she is trained.

I once saw a very handsome black gyrfalcon, captive bred and unhacked, who seemed incapable of landing or, indeed, stopping on her first free flight. She went on an on, at first at a great pace, but eventually going slower and getting lower and lower, obviously wanting to land. Fortunately we were able to follow her in a car. Eventually she tried putting her feet down, dragging them through scrub, but apparently with no idea how to lose speed, stall and land. Once or twice she touched the ground with a trailing foot or wing tip then suddenly she hit the ground hard, rolling over two or three times before coming to an untidy stop, and looking even more surprised than we were.

The unhacked hawk has little muscle and may well have to spend several days stooping at the lure, once she has learned to do so, before she is ready to try at quarry. The hacked hawk is fit and strong when taken up. Although fat and well she will have a natural hunger, as does a wild hawk, and so will be attentive at lesson time without having to reduce her condition. The unhacked hawk is often full of internal fat and in hot weather may be difficult to get into condition. The hacked hawk knows how to chase and may already have killed. She trains quickly and knows how to land, how to use the wind to her advantage and how to use her feet.

There are some disadvantages. Your hacked hawk may well be interested in chasing almost anything that flies in front of her rather than being completely directed to the one quarry you wish her to fly. She may well have learned to sit down on any perch, and trees or fence posts might prove a temptation when she is waiting-on. If flown close to where she was hacked she might well leave the falconer in anticipation of the food she would expect to find there.

One of the advantages is that the hacked hawk will happily fly along with another hawk, having done so daily at hack. Another is that she may have learned already that chasing wood-pigeons usually ends up in failure, with the pigeon safe in trees. Finally, being fit and strong the hacked hawk is likely to stay long enough on the wing, during those critical early days at game, to see game flushed under her before feeling tired enough to want to take perch.

If unhacked, the eyasses may be left in the breeding pens with their parents until they are hard-penned. Without actually catching them it is difficult to see if the last of the wax has come away from the growing primaries, but careful observation of the wing feathers as they cross over the tail should be indication enough. It is better to take eyasses from the wild only shortly before they fly from the eyrie. Some falconers have experimented with taking eyasses while still in the down, and by feeding them on the best of food they have hoped to produce extra large hawks. It is worth remembering that single eyasses in an eyrie are often rather larger than those from a clutch of four. However, there is no advantage in having an extra large falcon for grouse because they often take rather longer to get fit, which is a disadvantage to the average modern falconer who has a limited season on the grouse moors. There may be some advantage in having an extra large tiercel, although some of the best have been small.

If taken when still in the down, eyasses will require hand feeding, and might well become very noisy 'screamers', regarding the falconer as mother. Such hawks, surprisingly, are often good performers in the field, as was 'Bitch II', who screamed for the whole of her nine seasons as a trained hawk yet was a successful grouse hawk, taking 176 grouse in her last season, a feat unlikely to be bettered. However, a 'screamer' is something I prefer to do without. A friendly whine or the odd scream is pleasant to hear, but the continuous harsh call of a confirmed 'screamer' is hard to bear and does not endear a falconer to his neighbours.

Fig. 94 Gilbert Blaine's hack site at Tilshead in Wiltshire

Hack sites

There is almost as much discussion among falconers about the perfect hack site as to the advantages and disadvantages of hack. Gilbert Blaine, who stoutly supported the value of hack, wrote in *Falconry* (Allen, 1936):

> The best site for a hack house is against the side of a small copse, facing east or south, on some high down or open moor, in a quiet secluded spot removed from a high road, and off the beat of inquisitive prowlers. A position should be selected which affords a wide view of the surrounding country, and if there is a pond or stream of water not far distant where the young hawks can bathe, so much the better. A few old ragged fir trees in the copse make excellent roosting places for them at night.

Stephen Frank, who has hacked more hawks than any other falconer in Britain since the 1930s, used an old horse-drawn chaff wagon, one end of which was backed up against a large old oak tree on the west side of a copse on the family farm. The young hawks were turned out a few days to a week before they could fly. Within a day or two they would be clambering around on top of the hut or wagon and up into the trees, using the rough larch poles provided for that purpose. Thus they would learn to recognise the locality in preparation for when they started flying about the country. Within a week they would make their first clumsy flights and, to make sure that they were not at risk, any cattle or horses would be removed from the grass field around the hack place until the hawks were well on the wing. The first flight or two often ended in a crash landing in the field, when the hawk would invariably rush straight back to the hack house, half-flying, half-running, and quickly clamber back up the larch poles leaning against the house for that purpose, not feeling secure until safely home again. Because the young hawks do on occasion crash land in their early attempts at flying, it is important to make sure that there is no standing corn or other high crop within some hundreds of yards of the hack house.

Hack house at Tilshead, Wiltshire

Thoughts on training

Within a few more days the young hawks will be landing successfully on surrounding trees, walls, fences or buildings, and the larch poles should then be removed so that vermin cannot use them to get at the hawks or their food. Once the hawks are flying strongly there is little risk of loss, although there is some danger that an inexperienced hawk trying to bathe in a cattle trough or reservoir may not be able to get out again. To guard against this it is a good idea to have two or three portable hawk baths in the grass field near to the hack house. Also, until the eyasses are strong on the wing there is great danger from any wild goshawks that are breeding locally, and to hack in peregrine or eagle country could be hazardous.

Fig. 95 Stephen Frank's hack site at Quelfurlong Farm

Feeding at hack

The eyasses should be fed twice a day. Stephen Frank used to feed at about 7 a.m. and again at 6 p.m. On his hack wagon the feed, usually pigeon, rabbit, rook and so on, was tied securely to heavy boards. If the previous meal had not been cleared up, rather less would be tied for that meal. Sufficient portions were put out so that each hawk could feed separately. If any of the eyasses were very young the boards had to be placed in the bed of the wagon, but as soon as the hawks were branching the boards were placed across the top of the wagon. The boards could be

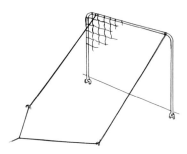

Fig. 96 Square bow-net set against a board, wall or tree trunk

removed, cleaned and replaced without the hawks clearly seeing the falconer. Always taking their food from these boards, the eyasses could be easily trapped at the end of their period of freedom with a bow-net set upright against the trunk of the oak tree and operated from the hide built at the front end of the wagon.

Colonel Blaine had logs of wood set up as feeding blocks in front of the hack house, one for each hawk. When trapping the hawks running nooses were set up on each block, with the lines running back to the hack house where the falconer would be lying in wait. However, these snares are easily disturbed by the hawk as it lands on the block, and it is better to use meat tied to a ring in the centre of a bow-net set out on the grass.

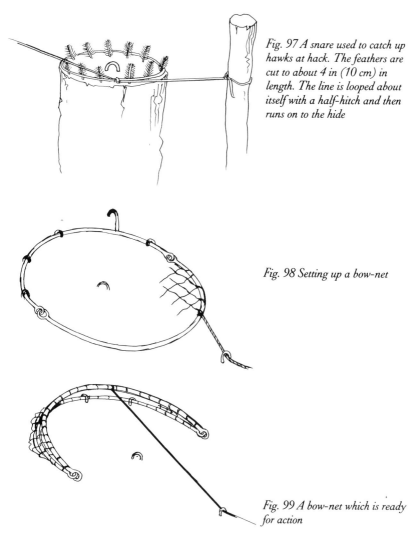

Fig. 97 A snare used to catch up hawks at hack. The feathers are cut to about 4 in (10 cm) in length. The line is looped about itself with a half-hitch and then runs on to the hide

Fig. 98 Setting up a bow-net

Fig. 99 A bow-net which is ready for action

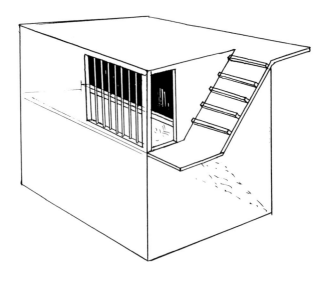

Fig. 100 A simple design for a hack house made of marine plywood

The modern hack house

A modern version of Blaine's hack house could easily be constructed from marine or exterior plywood. For additional security it could be set up in a farm wagon or on a low building. Initially the young hawks could be fed inside on the artificial nest, then, as they became more active, they could either be fed on boards on the roof or on logs set up in front of the house.

Bad habits

However securely the feed is tied to the boards or blocks, it is more than likely that the eyasses will carry off pieces of meat. This is all the more easily done if they are being fed on day-old chicks. It could be that they will then attempt to carry both lure and quarry when they are trained. But I suspect that careless handling when being entered to the lure and being lifted from the lure before they have enjoyed a reasonable reward, is more likely to teach a hawk this bad habit. After all, hawks reared in pens invariable carry their food from the feed shute to their favoured perch, but they do not appear to be more prone to carrying than other hawks.

Eyas activity

It is difficult to say whether the location of the hack place or the weather plays the greater part in determining how much activity there is among the eyasses. Presumably a hack site on a cliff top or mountain side where the prevailing winds create a continuous updraft, would encourage the eyasses to spend much of the day on the wing. Certainly in very still, hot weather the eyasses spend much of the day sitting about. But wherever the hack site is, on a windy, sunny day or in stormy weather the eyasses will spend all day soaring high under the clouds, and chasing and stooping at one another or at passing birds.

On such days it is marvellous to lie back in a comfortable deck chair with a good pair of binoculars and enjoy the wonderful display. While watching the eyasses it is sometimes possible to get an idea of the potential of the most easily identifiable of the hawks. To assist in this it is possible to mark them by, for instance, only putting a jess on the left leg of one hawk, or on the right leg of another. Different coloured leathers might be used, or fluorescent-coloured wide temporary rings. Traditionally, hawks were hacked handicapped with extra heavy hack bells. Bells might well be useful in warning a trigger-happy pigeon shooter that the hawk is not a passing pigeon, but on the whole it is better not to advertise the fact that you are hacking hawks in the neighbourhood (apart, of course, from discussing your plans with your land-owning neighbours). Certainly, to handicap your eyasses with heavy bells seems to defeat the very aims and objectives of hack.

Hacking from tall buildings

It is possible to hack hawks from the top of tall buildings, churches, cliffs or quarries. Major Stanley Allen hacked peregrines from the flat roof of the tower at his lovely home in Kent with great success. However, it is better not to release the eyasses until they are almost hard-penned and have spent some days in the bar-fronted pen. During this time they see and remember the landmarks around the hack site and when, during feeding, the front is quietly opened, pulled up with strings or some such arrangement, they are unlikely to wander far. Provided that the opening is sufficiently large the eyasses will continue to feed within the pen, and so can be caught up by simply dropping the bars back into place.

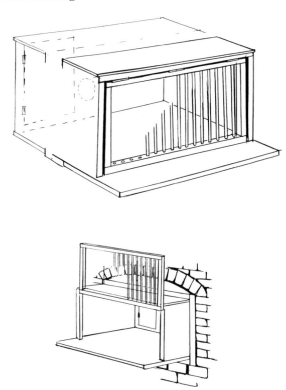

Fig. 101 A hack box for use in high buildings. The box may be fixed in an opening or window with access at the back

Lure hacking

Hawks can also be hacked to the lure. This can be done at ordinary hack, using one heavy lure for each hawk, rather than with food boards or 'blocks'. The only possible advantage of this method is that the hawk is already broken to the lure when taken up for training. The disadvantage would be that the hawks would certainly see the lures being thrown out by the falconer (for half the value of this method would be lost if they didn't) and, associating the falconer with food, might well start screaming at him. An alternative is to hack the hawk after it has been trained to the lure and manned. After flying the hawk for some days in the same locality she is left free. She soon becomes established in the area and is called to the lure once or twice a day for her rations. Some falconers using this method lure hawks in the evening, then take them up and put them into a house for the night before releasing them again in the morning. Others leave them at liberty night and day. Frici Pratesi kept a rather inferior peregrine at lure hack for more than a year, and how she could fly at the end of this time. She later became a fine grouse hawk whose stylish performances were enjoyed by many.

Duration of hack

The question of how long hawks should be kept out at hack is again the subject of much discussion. If one looks up what records are available, some successful hawks have enjoyed only two weeks' hack, for example 'Black Cloud', a Lundy tiercel that belonged to the Rev. Gage Earl Freeman, and 'Pip' a tiercel belonging to Dr Christian Saar. However, others have stayed out much longer: 'Sibella' for five weeks, 'Lundy III', 'Old Lundy' and his sister, 'June' for six weeks.

There is perhaps an argument in favour of a short hack of, say, two weeks or a long hack of six or seven weeks, rather than the often preferred four weeks of liberty. With a short hack the eyas will probably not have chased much in the way of quarry and so will not have been disappointed. With a long hack, although risking the loss of the hawk, there is every chance that she has made a kill or two. Once they have killed a few head of quarry there is little to hold them to the hack site, and even less chance of them coming in to feed when they may be caught. An older eyas might well continue to hang around the hack house if there are younger eyasses out with her. She might, of course, lure them away to her kills.

When tiercels and falcons are out at hack together it is important to remember that the more active and faster developing tiercels often succeed in killing before their larger sisters. However, although more backward, the falcons are stronger and easily drive their brothers from the kill. In the evening the tiercel will return to the hack house for his meal, while the falcon will be noted as missing by the watching falconer. At this critical time towards the end of hack, it is easy to assume that it is the missing falcon who has started killing for herself, and to make plans to catch her up while the real culprit is allowed a few more days' grace at some risk of losing him.

Catching up and trapping

Ideally, each hawk should be caught up in turn as soon as he or she is suspected of having killed. In practice, it is difficult if not impossible to be sure which hawk has killed, so if one or two have missed coming in to the hack house at feeding time, then it is better to catch them up as they come within the sweep of the bow-net. If some of the eyasses out at hack are from second clutches, and therefore are clearly younger and more backward, they can be easily recognised and left out longer.

Before snaring or netting a hawk it is important to check all surrounding trees and favoured perching places to make sure that no other hawk will see you trapping one of their companions. The sight of a hawk struggling in the net or snare, and of an excited falconer rushing forth from the hide to secure the trapped hawk, is more than enough to frighten off other hack hawks who may well not come back into feed for many days.

Thoughts on training

Gilbert Blaine records having to wait more than a week to trap a tiercel that had been frightened off by seeing a companion trapped. This was at a hack site at Black Hill above Bere Regis in Dorset in 1900. The tiercel would come over the hack house, flying very high and screaming, but wouldn't come down to feed. Eventually he suddenly came in, without any warning, on the following Sunday morning and so was caught. This tiercel was the first of many that Blaine got from Lundy, and he amply repaid the trouble he had been to take up from hack by killing 56 partridges in his first season in far from ideal country.

Use of the whistle

It is sometimes possible to net two eyasses at the same time if both are within the compass of a large bow-net, but it is rather more difficult to pull two snares at the same time. It is not wise to try and hack a hawk on its own. If you have a single eyas it is better to train it to the lure, then to lure hack it for as long as you dare. When feeding your hack hawks it is a good idea to blow loudly on your hawking whistle as soon as you have finished putting out the fresh food. The sooner your young hawks learn to associate the whistle with food the better, and this will also be helpful later on during training. Many trained hawks will come up to the shrill call of a whistle without the need for a lure.

Hacking where you intend to fly your hawks

It is debatable whether it is a good idea to hack your hawks where you will fly them later at quarry. However, the idea does have its attractions. The hawks will get to know the country so that if they are lost out hawking they will almost certainly return to the hack site to take stand for the night on a favourite tree or building. Even if the hawk has killed she will probably make her way back to the hack site the following day. Of course, this can become a confirmed habit which is very reassuring provided that the hawk doesn't start clearing off to her favourite area instead of waiting-on over your patient pointer or returning to the lure. If flown daily in the same country, many hawks will be little inclined to leave it, and indeed will return to it if lost on neighbouring ground. An old passage tiercel, who was flown for many seasons at rooks on the Wiltshire Downs, was always to be found perched in a favourite Scots pine if lost on a kill or in pursuit of quarry. In his last season he would sometimes refuse the rooks he had been slipped at and would go straight away to his tree where we would find him.

There is something to be said for hacking your hawk in very different country from that in which you propose to fly her. If you expect to fly her on a treeless grouse moor it might be an advantage to hack her where there are lots of trees. Thus, while at hack the hawk will naturally take stand in trees, but when taken on to the moor and finding none of her favourite perching sites, she may well be inclined to stay on the wing. Hacked on a grouse moor she will know all about rocky outcrops and fence posts and find them a welcome resting place.

Passage hawks

Of course many passage hawks trapped early in the season are little more experienced than a well hacked eyas. Some passage hawks have been trapped with down still on their heads and wing butts. Passage hawks and haggards which are late caught are, naturally, much more experienced in the ways of the wild. However, this is not necessarily of real value to the falconer, particularly if he wishes to use his hawk for the very specialised art of game hawking.

It is sometimes said by trappers from the Middle East that they normally only trap the worst hawks, the failures who have difficulty in finding their own living and who therefore fall easy prey to the trapper's lure. The hawks of the year are those that are trapped only when the skill and cunning of the trapper have been stretched to the utmost. Certainly many fine and excellent hawks *are* trapped, but it is nevertheless surprising how many are brought in that are poor in condition, with a claw missing, a broken toe or a scab or wound on their breast. Even so, it would be fair to say that most passage hawks are more skilled in flying and footing than the average eyas at the start of the season at quarry. Also, passage hawks or haggards are soon entered and suit a falconer who has only a few weeks' hawking a year. However, an eyas flown throughout the whole of the season will invariably fly as adroitly as many wild-taken hawks, and will certainly outscore them.

Passage hawks at game

Contrary to popular belief, not all passage hawks or haggards turn out well at waiting-on for game. In his book *Falconry* (Allen, 1936) Gilbert Blaine wrote:

> Better results may be obtained with passage hawks, of which the majority can be trained to wait-on during the time between the fall of the year, the season in which they are usually caught, and the following August, when they can be flown at game. They have more brains than eyasses, and are quicker in learning the advantage of position in relation to the wind, in expectation of grouse being flushed under them. Moreover, a really good one will outclass the eyas, both in the deadliness of her stoop and footing qualities, and in the superior style in which her every action is accomplished. So many eyasses straggle away downwind just when they are about to be served with grouse, and then have to face a long upwind flight without the force of a stoop behind them, in which the grouse has all the advantage. No passage hawk that has learned to wait-on for grouse is ever guilty of these bad tactics.

Thoughts on training

It is difficult to believe that Blaine could write the above when so few of the many passage hawks he tried at partridge and grouse proved reliable at game hawking, and were consistently outscored and outclassed by hacked eyasses. But some were of the finest class, such as 'Lady Jane', 'Rhoda' and 'Antoinette', the passage tiercels, 'Ready' and 'Gnome' and the haggard falcon, 'Dawn'.

Blaine wrote in his diaries of the many other hawks he tried. *August 22nd 1922;* '"Ariadne" [haggard falcon] put up two very bad performances, sitting down constantly, and was lucky in killing two grouse. Unless she improves she will not make a game hawk.' *August 24th;* '"Ariadne" sat down repeatedly and is quite hopeless as a grouse hawk.' *September 19th, 1924;* 'The haggard ["Flying Duchess"] did not go high enough and was outflown by an upwind grouse.' *August 26th, 1923;* '"Phoebe" [passage falcon] after a half-hearted attempt to catch a grouse in the morning, caught a common gull in the river after lunch.' *August 25th, 1913;* the passage falcon ["Gladys"] as usual refused to mount and after coursing and putting in a grouse, caught a rook. We have given up all idea of flying her at game.'

No doubt the passage hawk can fly with great style and has experience in footing her quarry in the wild, but she also has an interest in a wide variety of quarry and it will take far longer to turn her into a specialist who is only interested in the quarry you have chosen for her. She is less willing to leave quarry that she has put into cover, and will sit hoping that she may have another chance to fly at it rather than return obediently to the falconer who, if grouse hawking, might well have the dog still patiently on point with more grouse in front, ready to flush. If trapped in the Middle East a passage hawk will happily sit on the ground and throughout August and September she will be heavy in the moult. Despite this there have been some outstanding wild-taken hawks trained in recent times; 'Aurora', 'Lady St Sue', 'Dawn', 'Tremontana' and 'Elsevir' have all been falcons of the highest class, while the tiercels 'Dharif' and the tiny 'Naseem', were grouse hawks which were perfect in style and ability.

Early use of bells and telemetry

As soon as you take up your hawk from hack (the same would apply to a freshly-trapped passage hawk), in addition to hooding her and dressing her with strong, but soft, jesses, swivel and leash, it is just as well to put a bell on her so that she will grow accustomed to the furniture. During early training, the hawk has much to occupy her attention and will usually take little notice of jesses and bells. If not belled until later on in her training she might find the bewits and bells annoying, and so continually pull and bite at them. For the same reason it would be a good idea to glue a tail telemetry clip on to her deck feather straight away. Later, when you are carrying her you could clip on a tail-mounted or leg-mounted transmitter so that she becomes accustomed to the feel of it – this might well help you to find your hawk and not just her transmitter when you are flying her.

Hoods

It is better not to use a brand new hood on a young hawk, but to sort out a comfortable worn hood that fits well, does not let in light and does not come off when securely braced up. If comfortable, and not pressing around the nares, as many new hoods do until they have become moulded to the correct shape, the eyas will be less likely to scratch at the hood. I usually cut the buttons off the ends of the braces so there is no chance of the hawk catching a claw in the button. Unless you are very sure that she has no casting in her it is all the more important to use a hood that a hawk can cast through without difficulty. For the first few nights it is dangerous to put your young hawk on a screen perch, even in a darkened mews. It is far better to tie her with a short leash to a portable 'block' perch, a well padded box cadge or a strong cord tied around the middle of a large jute sack filled with sand. Tied like this in a completely blacked out room, the hawk can come to little harm should she bate or even get her hood off. If she does manage to do either of these things, slip into the room as quickly and as quietly as you can, and with the minimum amount of light, lift her and rehood her. Be careful when bracing up the hood: the hawk will not be used to being touched and may well turn and bite or strike out at anything she senses is close to her.

A friend who always used his tongue to get hold of the braces was severely bitten by a hissing eyas who turned and caught hold of his tongue. For some moments he leapt about, his tongue seemingly getting longer and longer, with blood spurting everywhere, until eventually I stopped laughing for long enough to reach over and touch the hawk on her shoulder, so making her let go in order to snap at the fresh distraction.

Feeding

The first priority with any hawk, whether a recently trapped passage hawk or an eyas from hack or a breeding pen, is to encourage her to feed. Hopefully she will have had little food, making it a good time to tempt her to feed as she will still react to being touched by hissing with an open beak and biting or snatching at anything rubbed against her feet. It is more important to get her to feed first before stroking her and getting her used to being touched. Once she is feeding freely and happily, then you can start handling her because she will have her mind on the food and will take less exception to being touched. Stroking her feet and the inside of her thighs is one of the ways to encourage her to get her head down and, hopefully, to start pulling at the strategically placed meat. Touch her too much before feeding lessons and she may well fail to react when necessary. However, a difficult hawk can usually be induced to bite, and eventually feed, by taking hold of her left foot (if on the left fist), pulling it down into the palm of your gloved hand and squeezing it between your fingers and the ball of your thumb. Feeling trapped, the hawk will try to bite what is holding her and, given time, will eventually swallow a snippet of meat. Once a hawk starts feeding (all long winged hawks will at first be fed through the hood, while short winged hawks and sometimes merlins are fed without the hood), she will invariably feed on further occasions provided that she is ready for a meal and that the way you present the food and the surrounding conditions is not suddenly different.

Some hawks, whether a passager or a recently snared hack hawk, will sit like a dummy if hooded and will not bate, hiss or react in any way to your advances. If unhooded, a hawk of similar temperament will either sit or bate off and hang, without flapping her wings, by the jesses. If you lift the hawk up she will refuse to use her feet, and will topple off to hang motionless again at the full length of her jesses. Such hawks are difficult to train. Far easier to cope with is the hawk that bates vigorously, puffs out her feathers, hisses or screams and grabs at anything that touches her. I believe it was one of the Mollen family who is said to have commented, 'All hawks can be trained but some are not worth the trouble.'

Early feeding lessons are best done with good quality food such as pigeon. Thus when the hawk does eventually take a snippet in her beak it will be to her taste, encouraging her to continue feeding. This is particularly true with haggards and some passagers. Once, in Arabia, one of the falconers was feeding a recently trapped haggard lanner for the first time. She was co-operative and soon was putting her head down to bite at the meat touching her feet. The falconer was using a lump of fresh mutton, but the falcon didn't like it and continually threw each snippet away. Luckily I found the leg of a houbara bustard killed earlier in the day and as soon as the meat was changed the falcon swallowed a piece and continued to feed, taking a good crop.

It is important to get wild-taken hawks, particularly haggards, to take as much food as possible in the early days after capture. Haggards quickly deteriorate in condition and so may become very susceptible to disease during this stressful period. A haggard or passager handled as soon as possible after trapping will be keen to feed at a set time each day. Wild hawks in good condition, used to a plentiful and healthy food supply, will be as eager for food as they were in the wild.

The well-hacked eyas has a natural hunger like the passage hawk, and will soon feed freely through the hood. However, the pen-reared eyas is more likely to be full of internal fat and so may well be more trouble, having little appetite to stimulate her. Do not overdo feeding through the hood; it is easy to encourage the tiresome habit of continually biting at the glove or jesses when hooded on the fist.

The correct way to hold a hawk

A hawk must learn to be comfortable and content on the hand and this is easier for her if she is held correctly. The jesses should be held between the thumb and the base of the first finger, with the swivel between the first and second fingers so that the button of the leash acts as a stop behind those fingers. The leash should then be wrapped firmly but not tightly once or twice around the base of the remaining fingers, with the spare end of the leash looped out of the way. However, a better and more sensible alternative for those occasions when you are 'manning' a hawk and are likely to be carrying her for some time, is to tie the spare end of the leash to the loop or tassle on the glove, or to a button hole or a bag belt. I usually tie the leash to my arm, leaving no loops or slack to get tangled up with the hawk should she bate.

The hand should be held upright (as if you were taking hold of a glass – not as if you were giving a horse a sugar lump) so that the hawk has a comfortable perch on the thumb and first finger. The arm should be relaxed so that it cushions any movement, and the forearm should be parallel with the ground. Some hawks are inclined to clamp their tails against the back of the glove and spoil the tail against the swivel and leash. If a hawk is inclined to do this then you should keep the swivel and leash button in the palm of the gloved hand and wrap the leash around the two smaller fingers but in the opposite direction. Occasionally a falconer is seen with the jesses held between first and second fingers. This is not only less secure but makes it more difficult for a bating hawk to recover its position on the glove. Nobody would expect to tie a hawk to a screen perch with the swivel below the top of the perch.

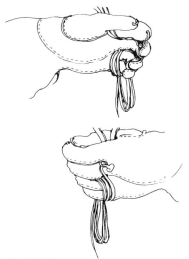

Fig. 102 The correct way to hold the jesses when carrying a hawk

Gyrfalcon feeding on the fist. Note the meat held in the correct position

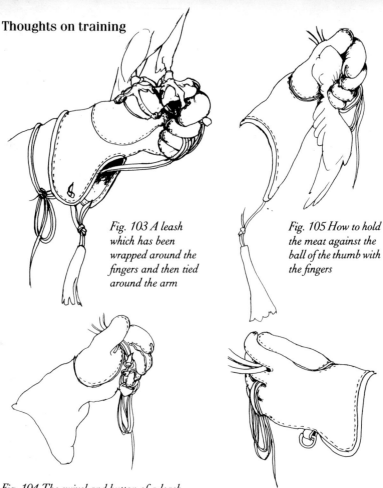

Fig. 103 A leash
which has been
wrapped around the
fingers and then tied
around the arm

Fig. 105 How to hold
the meat against the
ball of the thumb with
the fingers

Fig. 104 The swivel and button of a leash
held in the palm of the hand

Fig. 106 How not to hold the jesses

Feeding a hawk on the fist

When feeding your hawk hold the meat in front of your thumb, that is
against the ball of your thumb, and secure it with your three lower
fingers. You should be keeping the meat in place with the lower fingers
of your left hand, although at first this will feel as difficult and as
uncomfortable as holding the reins of a team of horses. Held this way the
meat is not all muddled up with the jesses, swivel or leash. It is also more
conveniently placed for the hawk to hold it firmly with her inner claws,
as she prefers, and to eat the meat in front rather than having to twist
herself around to reach meat back between her legs. If your hawk
'mantles' over her food, an unpleasant habit, keeping the food in its
proper place means that she is less likely to get her panel feathers mixed
up in her meat.

Early lessons

For the hawk's early lessons it is better to be indoors so that all is quiet. However, carrying your hawk is important if you are to accustom her to the movement of your arm as you walk about the garden. If it is windy, wait for a better day because the hawk may start opening her wings and 'jumping' on the fist as she feels the wind against her breast. This can easily become a habit and ruin an attempted approach upwind to a bevy of rooks in the hope of getting a closer slip. Rooks or crows will see the merest flicker of a wing and will fly away to safer skies before you can unhood your hawk.

It is traditional to stroke your hawk continually to aid in 'manning' her, but if you do this too much you could actually annoy her and make her more restless. If you must stroke her, it is as well to use a strong goose quill, a pencil or a stick. If she bites at your finger you will naturally react and pull the finger away which will only encourage her to bite again. If she bites something hard and unyielding she will soon be discouraged.

Hooding

Before unhooding a hawk for the first time it is good practice to touch her about the shoulders and head so that she will not take too much notice when you first undo or 'strike' the braces on the hood. Once you have undone the braces, leave them a moment and draw them closed again. The more a hawk is unaware of the braces being struck the better. It is important that she doesn't associate being touched about the head with the immediate removal of the hood. Far too many hawks get restless the minute they feel the falconer is about to unhood them. This restlessness can become so bad that it is difficult to unhood the hawk at all. The hood then has to be snatched off and the hawk reacts even more strongly to being hooded or unhooded.

After unbracing the hood, leave it for a moment then tilt it forwards to uncover the eyes before immediately easing it back into place. It is best to do this just before feeding, sitting quietly indoors in a darkened room with just sufficient light to enable you to see what you are doing and for the hawk to see the meat at her feet later on. A television in the corner of the room diffuses enough light. After partially unhooding her once or twice more, tighten the braces and encourage her to feed through the hood as before. It is important to remember to fasten the hood because otherwise it will fall off when the hawk bends down to her food. After she has taken a few mouthfuls, strike the hood again and smoothly take it off. For a moment or two time stands still and you hardly dare breathe. Then, with the slightest twitch of your gloved hand, you remind the hawk of the food and she will almost certainly continue to feed. For seconds at a time she will pause to stare at you. Do not look back directly at her until you sense that she will eat very little more. Then as you slowly lift the hood to her, look at her to hold her attention. As you hood the hawk, do up the braces and let her take a last few mouthfuls of food through the hood if she so desires.

You should hold the hood lightly by the plume or tag between the thumb and tip of your first finger. The other fingers lightly touch the side of the hood to hold it steady. If the plume is held in the fork of the thumb and finger there is a tendency to use the other fingers to tuck the back of the head into the hood. Don't push the hood on but round your wrist so that the hood sits lightly in place. Before presenting the hood to the hawk make sure that small pieces of meat or the braces do not get caught up inside the hood. If the hawk turns her head, touch her breast with the hood to make her look directly at it. If your hawk is inclined to sink her head into her shoulders or to sit back on her tail as you hood her, let your gloved hand sink backwards and down a little. This ensures that, in order to maintain her balance, the hawk will have to thrust her head forward into the hood.

Always use the hood as an artist would his brush. Think where you are putting it and do so delicately and with skill. If your hawk is well

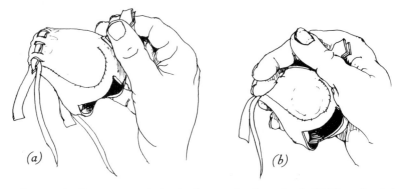

Fig. 107 (a) Fingertip control when hooding or unhooding a hawk. (b) Using the whole hand to hood a hawk

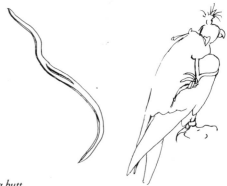

Fig. 108 A leather brail on a wing butt

trained to the hood there is no hurry to cram it on. A fast hooder is not necessarily a good hooder. It is always a pleasure to watch a good Arab falconer hood his hawk. Equally, though, a bad Arab falconer who is inclined to cram the hood on, pushing the head into the hood with his fingers, is a good example of how not to do it. Try not to catch up the chin feathers under the bill of the hawk with the throat lash of the hood; this will make her uncomfortable. If you do unhood the hawk then hood her again properly. A good hood should sit back in its correct position even when unbraced, but many hoods will not. If yours does then there is no great hurry to brace up the hood. Remember to take the hood off carefully. All too often, even among experienced falconers, hoods are snatched off, sometimes without even unbracing them.

It is good practice to open and close the braces occasionally without removing the hood. Every evening, when putting the hawks into the mews for the night, I walk along the line of hawks unbracing their hoods. Then, after a moment or so I walk back up the line to remove the hoods. If you unhood a hawk only when she is going to step to a perch, feed or fly, she will always anticipate you taking off the hood. She will be restless when you touch the braces and she will duck out backwards from the hood rather than let you unhood her. When tightening or loosening braces pull them with a smooth movement rather than jerking them and sink the hand slightly as you do so to make sure that the hood is not pulled forward.

As they become tame, some young hawks will go through a period of trying to evade the hood. Careful hooding and making sure that the hawk continues to finish her meal through the hood will usually overcome this. If she bates as you offer her the hood, wait until she has settled down again on the fist before offering the hood a second time. She will find it less easy to bate if you stand in the corner of a room and will be less likely to if the room is almost dark. Blaine advises 'brailing' your hawk, that is tying up her right wing with a leather brail, then hooding and unhooding her. Should the hawk bate she will have difficulty in regaining the fist and will have to be lifted back into place. She is then less likely to bate a second time. However, to have to use a brail is to admit failure.

With a really hood-shy hawk (these are made and not born), it is certainly worth changing the type of hood you have been using. 'Hai', a Peale's peregrine who had rather an unfortunate start in life, was impossible to hood until we changed to an Arab hood. Although she could never be called a perfect hooder, she certainly accepted the new hood and was little further trouble. One friend persevered for some years with placing titbits of meat inside the hood for a jerkin that would hood like an angel on the screen, but would bate violently outdoors if he thought he had not been given sufficient reward. This ploy, combined with another piece of meat for the jerkin after he had accepted the hood, certainly improved matters.

Flying to the fist

Within a few days your hawk will probably be stepping to your fist from the perch when approached at meal time. Whether she does so on the third or fourth day, or a week or so goes by before she condescends to come to you, doesn't matter. So much depends on the condition and temperament of the hawk and the skill and experience of the falconer. What is far more important is that you do not attempt to run before you can walk. A small improvement, with your hawk coming along slowly in the field without any setbacks, is far better than a great leap forward followed by a serious mistake which may leave its mark on the hawk throughout its trained life. It is better that the hawk should come to the fist immediately, if only from a foot or two away, rather than coming twice that distance after a long hesitation. Reward the hawk well and do not call her again; this is much better than having to call her over and over again for a smaller reward. This is equally true when you start calling the hawk to the lure. If she comes well and quickly, then let her eat all that is on the lure. Let her take her time and do not interfere and soon she will not need many titbits given from the hand.

Calling to the lure

The early lessons in coming to the fist will all be indoors, and it is not until the hawk will also feed bare-headed, hood quietly and come the length of the leash to the fist outdoors, that the lure is introduced. Your first lure can be a dead pigeon, or a small lure garnished with part of a pigeon, quail or partridge. Hold the pigeon or lure in your gloved hand and call the hawk to the fist as she has become used to doing each day. Squat down, close to the ground, and after letting her take a mouthful or two, toss the lure on to the ground a foot or so in front of you. She will almost certainly jump down on to it and continue her meal. The following day feed her a little from the lure at the fist again, then set her on a block perch and call her the length of the leash to the lure. Let her eat all that is tied to the lure, kneeling beside her but not interfering or offering her titbits unless she appears nervous or unsure of your presence. As she takes the last few mouthfuls from the lure put your gloved hand on top of the lure with a tempting piece of meat so that she can step up to the fist with no effort. For these early lessons it is probably worth while making a heavy, leaded lure that your hawk will not easily be able to drag or lift.

Deciding when first to put your hawk out to 'weather', unhooded on the block, is influenced by her behaviour and her willingness to jump to the fist. Most falconers, once their hawk comes the length of the leash to the fist, will first put her out to weather for half an hour or so before the normal feeding time. If she is at all nervous, it is better not to leave her and go out of her sight because she may bate wildly on your return. Sit down a little way away from her so that she doesn't forget you.

Hopefully, when you approach her, holding your fist so that she can see the proffered meal, she will step to the fist. Perhaps she may bate, but if you sit quietly she will eventually jump to the block and then the fist. If she bates violently scoop her up by the jesses and then try to settle her down, hooding her if necessary. I prefer not to put a hawk on the block unhooded until she is flying a few yards to the lure. If she has been brought gradually to the point where she comes boldly to the lure near you, she will be all the easier to call from the block after weathering.

Calling to the lure on the creance

Once your hawk comes to the lure the full length of the leash she will need to be called a greater distance on the 'creance' before you can trust her loose. The creance, a hundred yards or so of braided nylon line, should be tied directly to the slits in the ends of the jesses. The swivel should be taken off so that, if by some awful chance the creance comes undone, the hawk will not go away handicapped by the fact that her jesses are still held together by the swivel. If you rub some beeswax on the line the knots will hold better. The other end of the line should be anchored to a weight which is heavier than the hawk being flown. A hawk block laid on its side will roll if the hawk hits the end of the line and will ease her to the ground.

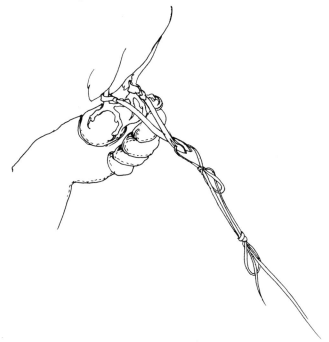

Fig. 109 A creance tied securely to the slits in the jesses

Of course the area chosen to call your hawk on a creance should be open, with no nearby trees or bushes, and the grass should be as short as possible because a creance will snag on the slightest thing, be it a thistle, a stone or a tuft of long grass. I use the local racehorse training gallops, with permission of course.

Call the hawk directly into the wind so that she comes directly to you and is less likely to snag the line. If it is stormy or there are very strong winds, do not fly her at all. Lay out the line to the movable anchor point rather more than half-way towards where you intend to drop the lure. Hopefully the hawk may never realise that she is secured because with luck and careful management she need never feel the pull as she overshoots the lure. Never let a hawk trail an unweighted creance behind her; this is both dangerous and unnecessary.

Flying your hawk loose for the first time

As soon as your hawk will come 60yd (55m) or so to the lure it is safe to try her loose. If you are in suitable country call her loose for the first few times in the same place as when on the creance. If you need to call her loose in different country call her at least once on the creance before you try her off the line. Do make sure that the meat is securely tied to both sides of the lure. Use a heavy lure or keep hold of the lure line, which should be of leather or a strong, braided nylon.

On one occasion a friend was calling his falcon loose for the first time. As soon as he swung the lure the falcon immediately started off from the gate where he had set her down. The lure line broke, the lure flew high into the air and the falcon bound to it, carrying it away over a hedge. Fortunately the falcon landed in the hack field and no harm was done on that occasion.

Remember to swing the lure until the hawk starts flying then let it drop to the ground as she approaches. Throw the lure out to one side and not directly at the hawk. Some hawks will not start towards you until the lure is on the ground. To overcome this call the hawk a short distance from a block to the lure, which should be dangling just above the ground. As soon as she takes hold, drop the lure to the ground. Call her once only and reward her well.

Flying to the lure

Before entering at quarry call your hawk over longer and longer distances; half a mile is not too far. After all, when out hawking it is usually when the hawk is a long way off that you need her to come to the lure. It is when she has put the quarry into cover at too great a distance for you to get there easily to re-flush it, or when she has been beaten high in the air in a ringing flight at a rook, that you need her to respond to the swing of your lure. A really long flight also teaches the hawk to look far afield for the lure or the quarry.

Some falconers stoop their hawks at the lure. With an unhacked eyas this may be useful for teaching her something of footing and how to use her wings. It also will improve her wind and muscle. However, with a hacked hawk that is already strong and fit from her four or so weeks of freedom, I can see little value in stooping at the lure. It is better to enter these hawks to quarry as soon as possible. A hawk that has been moulted in captivity is of course soft in condition and may well benefit from a course of stooping at the lure. However, with game hawks this is unnecessary. Old game hawks know the business and in anything like reasonable weather conditions they will mount to their pitch after a fashion. The game are also either old birds in the moult or young birds, thus because they are easy to catch a few long, stern chases will soon put an edge on the condition of the hawk. However, little harm is done if she

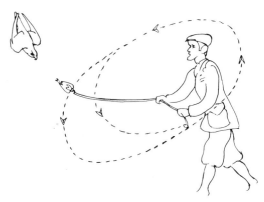

Fig. 110 Stooping a hawk at a lure with a long line

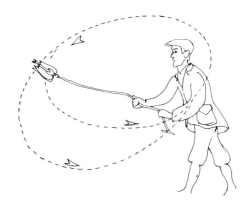

Fig. 111 Hold a long lure line with both hands apart

fails to kill for a few days. A rook hawk, particularly if it is to be flown at spring rooks, would benefit greatly from lure exercise. But it would also be good practice to call the hawk directly to the lure over a quarter of a mile or so and to reward her well.

Stooping a hawk correctly to the lure requires practice and is best learned by watching an experienced falconer. It is important to use a lure that is well padded and sufficiently heavy to swing well when the meat has been tied on, yet not so heavy that the hawk may hurt herself should she hit it. Should she do so, immediately drop the lure to the ground and let her have it. With a long lure line it is best to hold the line with both hands apart. Then, as the hawk approaches, slip the line through the right hand to give the additional length needed to lead the hawk through as it follows the swing of the lure. With a short lure line held in one hand the same can be done by extending the arm.

Some hawks seem very unwilling to strike at a swinging lure. To overcome this try swinging the lure on a short line attached to the end of a pole. By jerking it about just above the ground you might encourage an unenthusiastic hawk. Do not throw the lure high in the air, letting go of the line as you do so, and allowing the hawk to catch it in the air. This teaches her nothing and there is a great risk that the line might wrap around a wing or the body of the hawk, bringing her to earth with a bump if not worse. Leave such exhibitions to those people who feed off the sport and probably prize the adulations of an uninitiated crowd rather more highly than they do their hawk.

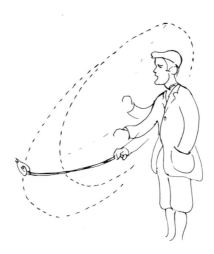

Fig. 112 Swinging a lure on a short line

4

Flying out of the hood

Rook hawking

Rook hawking as we now know it, that is spring rook hawking with long winged hawks such as peregrines, does not appear to have been practised to any great extent in earlier times. Early writers seem to regard the 'rook, crow and other vermin' as more suited to the goshawk. In those times the nobler flights at heron and kite provided the classic 'high flight' from the hood with peregrines and gyrfalcons. However, the crow was regarded highly enough to be listed as quarry in 1783 in the literature of the Confederate Hawks of Great Britain. Members of this club were the last to practise kite hawking and heron hawking in Great Britain.

By the 1860s Edward Clough Newcome (one time member of the Confederate Hawks of Great Britain and of the Royal Loo Hawking Club in Holland) still managed a few flights at heron near to his home in Norfolk, but by now rooks had developed as the main quarry for hawks flown 'out of the hood'. The Old Hawking Club maintained rook hawking as the main feature of their sporting year until the closing down of the club in 1927. Major Stanley Allen continued to fly spring rooks in the 1930s and J. G. Mavrogordato and others have done much to maintain the high standards set by their predecessors in flying spring rooks in recent years.

Certainly the best of the classic spring rook hawking was no mean substitute for heron or kite hawking. In open country strong, experienced rooks could test the speed, skills and adroitness of the best of the annual supply of newly trapped peregrines that were obtained every season from the trappers at Valkenswaard near Eindhoven in Holland. The Old Hawking Club would send the club's falconers and the hawks down to Wiltshire in February both to get the hawks entered and to have everything ready for the arrival of the first members in March. Hawking then continued into May, when hot weather, growing crops and the danger of hawks killing young rooks in their nests put an end to sport until the following season.

Autumn and winter rook hawking

Rooks can, of course, provide exciting sport in the autumn and winter, but there is less likelihood of a high, ringing flight. Indeed ringing flights are rare enough in the spring. Too many easy kills of young rooks and heavily moulting old rooks in August or September, or weak, hungry rooks in the hard weather of January or February, might well spoil promising young hawks and so prevent them from persevering at the more difficult spring rooks. Hawks all too quickly learn that some rooks are easier to kill than others, and they will then confine their attentions to such rooks. However, in modern times where falconers must, on the whole, confine their attentions to eyas hawks rather than wild-taken passage hawks, it is necessary to enter the hawk in the autumn, that is unless she is to be used for a season at game before changing her to rook hawking, a practice advocated by Stanley Allen. In the 1930s some of Allen's best rook hawks were well hacked eyas falcons that had been flown for a season at grouse by his friend Colonel Gilbert Blaine on Islay.

Flying passage peregrines at rooks

In the days of The Old Hawking Club the passage peregrines, used almost exclusively for their sport, were trapped in October or November and trained on during the winter. Thus they were conveniently ready for the start of the season in February or March. There is no doubt that these passage peregrines were perfect for the wild weather conditions of the average spring on the Salisbury Plain, and many high flights were enjoyed in pursuit of tough old 'cock' rooks passaging back to the rookery from far flung feeding grounds. It should not be thought that all flights were classic ringers for, although they were not handicapped as we are today by barbed wire fences and increasing woodlands, lambing folds were scattered over the Plain, encouraging many a rook to seek sanctuary. During the 1960s I was fortunate enough to be able to bring in some fine passage peregrines from the Middle East. These falcons were fit and strong from a season's 'houbara' hawking and, because they were imported before the days of licences and isolation restrictions, they could be entered immediately to rooks. What excellent sport we enjoyed! Now, once again the peregrine is freely and commonly available in the Middle East and there is no sound conservation reason why a few should not be imported as in earlier times.

Flying eyas peregrines at rooks

However, a well-hacked eyas would make a very acceptable alternative to the traditionally used passage hawk. The Old Hawking Club occasionally found an eyas peregrine that would take rooks just as well as its wild-taken brethren; 'Christmas', flown at rooks in 1922 was one such hawk. Peregrines, sakers, sakrets, and jerkins have all been flown at rooks with success and the occasional lanner and prairie falcon have also proved that the rook is not beyond their powers. The female gyr might also prove suitable for rooks, but she is perhaps too large and is less handy than the smaller hawks when it comes to performing well at what is an active and evasive quarry. The gyr might do better confined to crows or the larger gulls.

Whatever hawk is chosen it will be to the peregrine that the falconer turns for regular and reliable success in the field. The tiercel peregrine is probably too small to be regularly used at rooks. Some tiercels take rooks and take them well, but the rook is a tough and ugly customer on the ground and can inflict a great deal of damage with his long and powerful beak and his sharp claws. When caught crows are an even greater danger, and a friend once had a fine but inexperienced falcon blinded by a hoodie crow.

As always there are exceptions to every rule. 'Druid', an eyas tiercel of 1863 belonging to Cecil Duncombe, was entered to magpies but transferred his attentions to rooks and for three seasons took his turn with the passage hawks of the Old Hawking Club on the Plain. Edward Clough Newcome had a very fine rook hawk in 'Will-o'-the-wisp', a passage tiercel of 1838, and 'Plenipotentiary' ('Aladdin') a passage tiercel of 1876 was much admired for his style by the members of the Old Hawking Club although he only actually caught three rooks. More recently 'Cairo', an old passage tiercel of mine, took many spring rooks in the finest style to the delight both of his owner and his many admirers.

The only noticeable advantage of flying a tiercel at rooks is that one generally enjoys a greater number of ringing flights. Many rooks seem more confident about trying to outfly a smaller hawk. Sakrets, although a little larger than peregrine tiercels, are less likely to be damaged, because with their longer legs they can hold the rook further away from themselves and also keep well clear of the stabbing beak. It therefore follows that in searching for quality high, ringing flights it might be better to try females such as brookei or tundra (smaller sub-species of peregrine) than Peale's peregrines, large sakers or gyrfalcons.

Sakers as rook hawks

Although Alfred Frost flew a saker at rooks as early as 1889 in Cambridgeshire (the saker belonged to Captain C. W. Thomson), it wasn't until the 1960s that Jack Mavrogordato perfected the use of passage and haggard sakers, trapped by himself, for spring rook hawking. The majority of these sakers provided excellent sport and entertained the very many guests who enjoyed Jack's kind hospitality at Tilshead. Sakers are clever with their feet and they mount and stoop well and with great accuracy. However, they are not as fast as the best peregrines and do not cut into a rough head-wind in the same way. Their large wings, often an advantage, can be a handicap in strong winds. They are very persevering in pursuit of their quarry and will hunt to a great distance, being very loath to give up the chase as long as there is the smallest chance of success. However, they have an unpredictable temperament, changing in seconds from a tame, dog-like obedience to a nervous, panicky wildness.

Gyrs as rook hawks

Few gyrs have been flown at rooks in this country. A passage jerkin, trapped by John Pells in Iceland in 1845, took both rooks and partridge. A haggard Norwegian jerkin, 'Adrian', trapped at Valkenswaard in 1877 for the Old Hawking Club, was also flown at rooks. This haggard was some trouble to train but it was written of him that, 'He was entered to rooks on Salisbury Plain, and turned out a most splendid hawk, one of the grandest fliers the Club has ever possessed. Yet when hot weather set in he fell off in style, and refused to fly.' The records show that he only killed three rooks and was lost the following first of October from the moulting loft. Mavrogordato also had some success with his very handsome eyas Icelandic jerkin, 'Jack Spot'. The power, speed and activity of jerkins should make them ideal rook hawks, and now that they are widely available from captive breeding projects perhaps a few more will be given the opportunity to show what they can do.

Gyrs do not seem willing to hunt rooks without careful entering, but they do have a natural inclination towards the pursuit of game. Lanners have caught spring rooks successfully. Mavrogordato enjoyed some interesting flights with a cast of two lanners, one being the well known and loved 'Pearl'. A haggard Libyan lanner belonging to two boys at Marlborough College in the 1960s was a successful hawk. Both flew and caught rooks in the finest style. It should be remembered that the larger falcons can carry a rook with ease (sakers in particular can carry surprisingly heavy quarry), but this should not be of any consequence provided that the hawk has been trained and handled correctly.

Good hawks

J. G. Mavrogordato, who has written of rook hawking in both his own book, *A Falcon in the Field* (Knightly Vernon, 1967) and in Woodford's, *A Manual of Falconry* (A & C Black, 1987), said that good rook hawking requires three ingredients: good country, good hawks and good slips at the quarry.

If they are of a suitable species most hawks are potentially good, and it is up to the falconer to give them the opportunity to become successful at their intended quarry when training, entering and flying them. However, without good country there is little chance of high flights, and any rooks killed will have to be hunted from cover to cover rather like magpie hawking. Undoubtedly many rooks and crows can be killed in this manner in the most enclosed of country if assisted by active falconers. Hunted from bush to bush, dodging each stoop with a well timed flop into yet more cover, the flights can be great fun with the whole field participating. Particularly in the autumn, very large bags can be filled in this manner, but it does not compare with the sort of flight likely to follow a long slip in open country at a passaging rook in a wild north-east wind. Even in good country all too often a potentially good flight is spoilt by a barbed wire fence, a tractor working in a field or even by the rook making for cover under the very vehicle from which the falcon was slipped.

Good country

Unfortunately, suitable country becomes harder to find as the years go by. The Salisbury Plain, once the Mecca for generations of rook hawkers, has been altered out of all recognition. As early as 1900 the members of the Old Hawking Club were sadly reporting the inroads that the military were making on the Plain with the construction of camps, railways and ranges. Since then these tin and wood camps have become permanent garrison towns, and the ever-increasing military manoeuvres, involving the live firing of ever bigger and further reaching weapons, have all but closed down the Plain. In addition, the continuous planting of more and more copses and woods to create better training facilities (which does not return the Plain to how it was as is so often claimed by the authorities) has greatly altered the appearance of the open downland beloved by Fisher, Lascelles, St Quintin, Heywood Jones and Blaine. Much of the remaining downland in Wiltshire, Berkshire, Dorset and Sussex is also spoilt by wire fences, tree belts and the growing number of other people also enjoying the countryside. The changing farming pattern, with the increase in winter-sown corn and oil-seed rape, makes it difficult to hawk into April or May. Better country could probably be found in the East of England where 'prairie' farming has opened up vast tracts of country.

Good slips

Before you slip your hawk at her first rook it is important to have her fit and obedient to the lure. However, if you intend to enter your eyas hawk to autumn rooks it is better not to do too much work at the lure, but to enter her to the quarry as soon as possible. Certainly, if a hawk has been hacked she can be entered to rooks as soon as she will come 600 yd (550 m) or so to the lure. If your hawk has been out of work for some time, has been moulting or is unhacked, it may be necessary to stoop her at the lure for some days to build up some muscle. It is important to remember that a thin hawk cannot fly strongly, while a hawk in good condition will fly tolerably well even if a little on the fat side and unfit. It is always a surprise to see how strongly unfit sakers will pursue their quarry in the desert, even though they may have done little or no flying for some months. These hawks, far from being thin, are indeed as round as when they were trapped many weeks before.

If a falconer so wishes he can spend some weeks getting a wild-caught hawk fit by stooping her at the lure. However, while it is inadvisable to waste so much time with an eyas, it is entirely unnecessary to do so with a hacked hawk. The time would be better spent getting the hawk to stoop at the real thing. Rather than stooping your hawk at the lure for the last few days before you hope to enter her to rooks, it is better to call the hawk to a dead rook or a rook-wing trimmed lure a quarter of a mile or so from your assistant. If the hawk is accustomed to coming from a great distance to the lure there is little risk of losing her should she fail to kill on her first few essays at rooks, even should she chase them to very distant cover. If a hawk is only ever called short distances to the lure or is thrown off to stoop at the lure, she will tend not to look far afield, so that when she is being introduced to rooks she will frustrate the falconer by seeming to ignore anything which is not immediately at her feet. If rooks are difficult to approach, making it necessary to slip your hawk from a car even on her first introduction, it is advisable to prepare the hawk for this by calling her to the lure and slipping her from the open window of the car as if slipping at quarry. It is important that every effort is made to reduce the strangeness of the situation to a minimum when entering.

Entering to rooks

I have yet to meet any wild-caught peregrine or saker that did not at least have a go at rooks when first shown them, provided that she had been flown to a rook-wing trimmed lure. Some eyasses may prove more difficult to enter, but if they are lured with and fed up on warm, recently shot rooks and if they are not too interested in the lure, they will be tempted usually by a small group of nearby rooks. Rooks following a tractor at the plough are often so engrossed in their greedy feeding that they take little notice of a Land Rover getting closer and closer, and indeed often don't see the falcon until she is nearly among them. Rooks following a plough often, however, appear in great numbers and are accompanied by jackdaws, seagulls and even pigeons.

Good slips are the key to success at rook hawking. Badly chosen slips, in which the rooks easily beat your hawk to cover, or where they are so close that they are away down wind before the hawk can command them, quickly encourage the hawk to search for other quarry or to self-hunt, ignoring the intended quarry to go off in search of rooks of their choice. In these days of telemetry there is every chance that you will find your hawk, perhaps even on a kill. However, this is not rook hawking. After all, the whole purpose of hawking is to watch the flight and hopefully see a rook caught in style by your falcon.

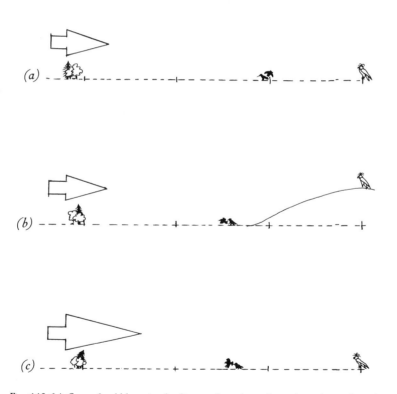

Fig. 113 (a) Cover should be twice the distance from the rooks as the rooks are from the falconer. (b) Where the falconer has a height advantage, the rooks can be nearer to cover upwind. (c) With a stronger wind the rooks can be nearer to cover upwind, but they need to be further away from side or down wind cover.

Flying out of the hood

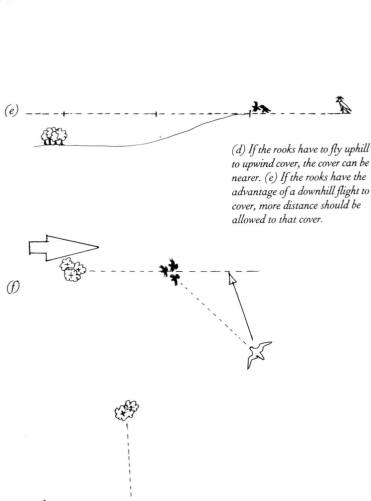

(d) If the rooks have to fly uphill to upwind cover, the cover can be nearer. (e) If the rooks have the advantage of a downhill flight to cover, more distance should be allowed to that cover.

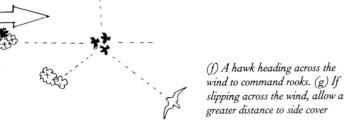

(f) A hawk heading across the wind to command rooks. (g) If slipping across the wind, allow a greater distance to side cover

Slipping into the wind

The first rule in slipping your falcon at rooks is to slip her into the wind, that is with the rooks directly upwind of you. How far upwind depends upon the experience and ability of your hawk, the strength of the wind, the proximity of cover such as trees, hedges, bushes or farm buildings, and whether the rooks are on the ground feeding or flying on passage. Except when attempting to enter an unenthusiastic hawk, do not slip at rooks too close to you; 150yd (135m) or so should be regarded as the minimum. If the slip is closer than this, the rooks are around the hawk and away down wind before the hawk is into her stride. Once the hawk is really wedded to her quarry, longer and longer slips can be attempted, provided that there is enough open country to allow the hawk to fetch the rooks before they get to cover. A really experienced hawk can easily take on slips of a quarter of a mile or more. Extremely long slips do not often produce a good flight, and if they do the flight may well be too far away to be enjoyed by the spectators. The falcon will often be able to get herself into a commanding position before the rooks notice her, so spoiling the chances of a sporting flight. It is commonly held that the distance to cover upwind of the rooks should be twice that which the falconer is from the rooks.

Although rooks should ideally be upwind of the falcon when she is slipped, it is not always possible to get a flight without stretching the rules a little. The reason for slipping directly into the wind is that rooks do not easily press forward into a head-wind. Peregrines and gyrs in particular can cut into the strongest of winds. Of course, once the falcon is over the rooks they will attempt to break away down wind, and if they do the flight will drift back towards the falconer who can then enjoy the flight. With a down wind slip there is every likelihood of the flight going on and on down wind until lost to view. However, when there is little or no wind the direction of the slip is not so critical. Equally, a clever hawk that flies with its head as well as its heart can quickly learn to adjust its position from a side-wind slip, angling across the wind before pressing forward into it.

Knowing your 'country'

It is important to know your country well, so time spent in reconnaissance, checking where the trees and bushes are, what crops are growing, where the rookeries are and where the rooks are feeding, is time well spent. Before slipping your hawk, consider what cover there is down or across wind from the rooks that you intend to fly. This reconnaissance is particularly important on rolling downland because quite a large copse of trees can be hidden in a fold in the hills. Check with binoculars that there are no rooks or other temptations down or across wind that might tempt your hawk from the chosen slip. It is worth taking the trouble and driving some distance if necessary to flush any rooks that could spoil a flight. Big flocks of rooks are often mixed with jackdaws, crows or pigeons, so you should check with binoculars before flying an inexperienced hawk. Once well wedded to rooks there is less need to worry because your hawk will not be easily tempted elsewhere. Single rooks (which on closer inspection are usually crows) are likely to be tough, confident old birds that will take a lot of catching or else just sick, unhealthy rooks.

Time spent in choosing the right slip in the right place for a particular hawk is the key to success. Later, if your hawk is good enough you will want to fly at passaging rooks. Again, time spent with binoculars will soon show where the regular flight lines are, for example where rooks are crossing back and forth from the rookery to feeding grounds. With luck the rooks will have to cross suitable open country, leaving sufficient room for a flight. When slipping at a rook on passage which already has some height advantage, a great deal of open country is required to ensure a worthwhile contest. The Old Hawking Club used a tame eagle-owl to lure rooks to suitably open country. The owl was pegged out on a tall perch and within moments rooks would start to mob it. J. G. Mavrogordato also used eagle-owls to great effect, but their use is now illegal.

Further advice on slipping

When slipping a hawk at rooks do not snatch the hood off and throw her at the rooks. Unbrace the hood well before you hope to slip her and, provided that she has been correctly trained, she should still sit quietly on the hand. As you approach the rooks the movement of a hawk flapping her wings is enough to send them scurrying off to the nearest cover. If you are on your feet it might be possible to creep up out of sight of the rooks behind the cover of a rick or a tractor. Alternatively, you could walk towards them, sheltering the hawk from view behind a companion.

If your hawk is fitted with Aylmeri-type jesses she can be flown either with 'field' jesses slipped through the eyelets or, better, with no trailing jesses at all. If you choose the latter option it is essential to have some means of holding the hawk until the hood it taken off. The simplest method is to have a long strip of leather (a leather bootlace is ideal), one end of which is attached to the glove. When the first jess is taken out of the eyelet on the ankle the leather bootlace is slipped through and the spare end is wrapped around the little finger of the gloved hand. The second jess can then be removed and both the jesses and the swivel may be slipped on to the hawk leash to keep them safe. In this way there is no danger of a hooded hawk getting loose. Only very silly falconers ever allow a hooded hawk to sit untethered. If a hawk ever does get loose when hooded, immediately call her. If you are in a car bang on the door panels until, hopefully, the hawk slowly flutters to the ground instead of damaging herself by flying into something. I remember a visiting falconer once slipping one of Mavrogordato's sakrets at a rook while she was still hooded. All of Jack's hawks were well trained to the whistle and fortunately the sakret immediately turned and flew back to the familiar blast of the whistle, alighting near to the hawking car. An alternative is to use a scissor dog-lead clip, again attached to the glove by a length of leash, which can be clipped to one of the Aylmeri eyelets.

Once in position it is often worth waiting to unhood your hawk until one or two rooks fly in to join those on the ground upwind of you. The movement will catch the eye of your hawk rather more than the rooks already sitting still on the ground. When feeding, one of the rooks will often flap two or three yards to join other companions and such a movement will often trigger your hawk into action. Do not throw the hawk at the rooks. Unhood her quietly and let her take off when she is ready. If she doesn't want to go there is absolutely no point in throwing her at them. When the hawk is more experienced then, if flying a passaging rook, by all means encourage her to take off quickly by launching her gently into flight.

Fig. 114 A leather lace or leash may be used to hold a hawk securely without jesses in Aylmeri eyelets

As the hawk leaves the fist, keep quiet and still. A shout at this moment might distract her from the intended flight, particularly if you have been in the habit of shouting to her as she comes to the lure. This is particularly so with a hawk that is new to the business. Indeed a shout might well alert the rooks a second or so before they see the falcon, and with a young hawk that second may well be vital in determining whether or not she succeeds. Also, do not set off in pursuit immediately but stand still and watch. You will be able to see more and therefore determine where the flight might swing; for example towards a small bush to which you can hurry to help your falcon or, as so often happens, coming back directly towards you. Don't leave it too long before using your binoculars because the further the birds are the more difficult it is to find them with the binoculars. It is far better to use binoculars when the birds are still relatively close and to keep watching them until the end of the flight.

Approaching rooks

In new country a falconer might be able to approach rooks on foot for a day or two, but the rooks will soon become suspicious and move off as soon as the falconer appears on the horizon. To get within reasonable range of rooks it is advisable to use a suitable cross-country vehicle, such as a Land Rover, from which the hawk can be slipped from an open window. Jack Mavrogordato went to much trouble to have a hatchway cut in the roof of the canvas tilt on his Land Rover so that a hawk could be slipped without the vehicle coming to a halt. He also had it painted to match the military vehicles that the rooks on the Salisbury Plain were accustomed to seeing every day. Jack even claimed that the rooks could differentiate between a diesel and a petrol engine, so like the military Jack had a petrol engine in his Land Rover. The hawking Land Rover was very similar to the military models and I well recall on one occasion driving over a brow of the downs near Imber with Jack at the tiller, only to be confronted with a mock battle in full flood. On we drove as soldier after soldier snapped to attention, saluting the Land Rover and its occupants whom they presumably thought were high-ranking officers.

Mavrogordato also equipped his Land Rover with a small wind sock (a small flag or pennant would suit just as well) and a Beaufort scale wind-gauge. The first is useful in determining the direction of the wind before slipping your hawk. The second is probably sensible, but in some seasons you would never fly at rooks if you were too influenced by borderline conditions.

Rooks certainly recognise individual vehicles, and if it is necessary to fly your hawks repeatedly on the same piece of ground, then use a borrowed vehicle occasionally.

Fig. 115 A Land Rover with a roof-hatch and a wind sock

What to do when the rook reaches cover

If the rook or crow should put into cover an immediate decision needs to be made as to whether to take the hawk down to the lure because there isn't much hope of reflushing the quarry, or to rush down to make every effort to serve the hawk again. If the 'put-in' rook is not too far away, and the cover is small, it is probably worth while to try to flush the rook out, because the falcon will learn quickly that you are helping her in so doing. However, if the cover is distant or extensive it is better to take the falcon down and to try again later in the day. Leaving a wild-caught hawk or a keen young eyas circling about is tempting providence, because the hawk may see other quarry away in the distance and so get lost. With the help of telemetry the hawk should be found without too much trouble, but she will have learned that she can search for and hunt quarry of her choice and so a promising rook hawk will be on the road to ruin.

Having been put into cover a rook, and even more so a crow, will be very loath to leave it, and will repeatedly return to its shelter given any chance to do so. However, a rook that has been hit by a hawk or has momentarily been held but escaped from the hawk's grasp, will very often take to the air and do its very best to outfly the hawk. Another disadvantage of leaving a hawk when she has put quarry into distant cover rather then luring her down, is that she may take perch. If you can get to close cover quickly there is every chance that your falcon will still be on the wing, circling above the cover in a good position to renew her attack should you manage to drive the rook from the cover. Do try to flush the rook in this situation, ideally flushing the rook upwind or away from even better cover.

When your hawk takes her rook by all means shout to the world that she has succeeded. Get to your hawk as soon as possible, particularly if she has taken a crow. There is every likelihood that the crow's mate will come up and deliberately attack the hawk in an attempt to rescue the other. A falcon belonging to a friend of mine was blinded in this way. Rooks will also give a hawk a rough time, twisting feathers and stabbing at the hawk, right up until the breathless falconer is suprisingly close. More often rooks will mob up over the kill, cawing and creating a great fuss, with the more adventurous among them stooping at the hawk below.

Both rooks and crows will fight bravely and, unless a hawk quickly learns to get hold of the quarry by the head as soon as they land together, she will surely get damaged sooner or later by a stabbing beak. If she is too roughly handled your hawk might well start refusing to fly at such unpleasant quarry. Tiercels in particular are in great danger if they don't immediately get hold of their rook properly, but those few tiercels that proved to be top-class rook hawks seemed to understand how to wrap up their quarry, one foot muzzling the head while the other foot holds one or both of the quarry's legs. Reward your hawk well. Despite what has been written by the old masters I have yet to come across a peregrine or a saker that did not enjoy rook or crow flesh, although one gyr I know of would happily eat rook meat but turned her nose up at crow flesh.

Obedience

The belief that rook hawks need to be sharp in condition is not supported by experience. Once well entered and wedded to a quarry, the stronger the hawk is, the better she will perform. Her condition need only be tempered by the degree of obedience required to ensure that she will return to the lure if unsuccessful. However, if she is killing day after day a hawk can become careless of the lure and it is probably good practice to call her to the lure on occasion to remind her of the generous reward she will receive on responding. Some passage hawks, or haggards in particular, will be very obedient to the lure and yet, if flown at a rook which they lose in cover, will be very reluctant to return to the lure. They want to kill and seem little interested in the lure which they would normally return to as soon as it was shown to them. Such hawks are easily lost for they will surely see more rooks in the distance and go further and further away from the pursuing falconer. Even if found with the telemetry receiver there is every chance that they will have taken a full crop and will not be easy to take up. Extremely careful selection of slips is the only answer with such hawks, that is until you lose them!

It is clear that a rook hawk should be well trained to the lure and should come to the swung lure from a great distance. A game hawk rarely flies as far from the falconer, and in any case she will quickly learn to come back to the falconer without luring in expectation of further game being flushed for her. The rook hawk has no such encouragement to return in search of her master. If she does, lure her down and reward her well.

Flying a cast of hawks at rooks

In the days of the Old Hawking Club it was the practice to fly a 'make-hawk' together with the young entry, that is the new hawk of the season, when first entering to rooks. A make-hawk is an experienced rook hawk that is slipped at the quarry first, with the young hawk being slipped in behind her to join in the flight. With two hawks a rook is normally easily taken, and so the young hawk should not have a difficult flight or be disappointed. However, it is necessary to make sure that the make-hawk is not jealous of company and will not turn and see off her young trainee. At the same time the falconer also has to be careful that the young hawk is not so aggressive that she prefers to pursue the old hawk rather than the intended quarry, thus perhaps damaging an old favourite. Wild-caught hawks and hacked eyasses are less likely to turn on a companion. When flying hawks in a cast it is most important that the falconers are sufficiently experienced to slip and to follow the flight of *both* falcons. To slip the second falcon requires careful timing, in order to try and ensure that they both stay on the same rook. Do not slip a cast at a scattered flock, and only slip the second falcon when the make-hawk has already selected her intended victim. If both hawks stick to the same rook, then watching both hawks is straightforward. However, if they divide there is some risk that everybody will watch the same hawk and the other will be lost.

On one occassion when grouse hawking in Sutherland, the whole field were delighted to see three peregrines waiting-on over the pointer, 'Queenie'. The grouse were flushed and both the wild hawks and 'Old Bitch' stooped at the covey. However, everybody watched the stoop nearest to us which ended out of sight over a ridge, and it wasn't until somebody asked whether it was 'Old Bitch' or not that we realised that nobody had watched either of the other hawks. Fortunately 'Bitch' had the not unpleasant habit of screaming quite loudly on seeing an approaching falconer, and on spreading out we quickly found her sitting on her grouse in a circle of feathers in quite the opposite direction to the flight we had all so keenly watched.

It is surprising how rarely any damage is done to either hawk even should they disagree over who deserves the kill. Very often an intermewed hawk (that is a trained hawk which is moulted in captivity), as a make-hawk generally is, will step back off a kill if the young hawk is aggressive towards her. Intermewed hawks have become accustomed to feeding near to other hawks either at the block or in the moulting lofts. A well garnished lure or, better, another recently killed rook strategically positioned, will soon separate the hawks, allowing them to recover their composure and feed up in peace. However, on the whole a make-hawk should not be necessary to enter the average hawk to rooks.

Crows

Crows, whether carrion or hoodies, are more easily taken by a willing hawk than rooks. They are not so agile in the air and are less likely to take to the air, preferring instead to make for the nearest cover. Once there, provided that they can be re-flushed they are easily taken by a hawk waiting overhead. However, they are certainly more dangerous once taken and fight to the very last. Many good rook hawks will refuse crows. If correctly approached, few landowners will refuse you permission to fly your hawks at rooks, but they will positively welcome you with open arms should one of your hawks take crows.

Jackdaws

Jackdaws are now more numerous than I can ever remember and invariably any mob of rooks is sure to include a number of jackdaws. The jackdaw is extremely active on the wing and easily evades the stoops of all but the most adroit of falcons. 'Mansour', a very fine old passage peregrine took more than a few jackdaws as 'various' when rook hawking, but she rather spoilt this record by usually carrying her kill. No doubt if jackdaws could be found away from rooks they would prove an excellent quarry for first-rate tiercels, but this usually happens in unsuitable country. Seagulls would be better quarry for a tiercel.

Seagulls

Herbert St Quintin, a member of the Old Hawking Club, was the first falconer to make a special effort to perfect the training of peregrines for flights at seagulls in the 1880s and 1890s. At first he was convinced that only the very best passage tiercels were up to these flights, and he ordered annually the cream of the tiercel catch from Adrian Mollen in Valkenswaard. Later he was to use eyas tiercels and eyas and passage falcons, but he considered that tiercels provided the better sport. He invariably flew a cast of hawks at gulls and enjoyed success with all possible combinations, including tiercels with falcons and passagers with eyasses. However, his most successful casts were either two passage tiercels or a passage and an eyas tiercel. Another member of the Old Hawking Club, Colonel Gilbert Blaine, also found that gull hawking was a rewarding and exciting flight. He flew falcons, eyasses, passagers and haggards at gulls in the 1920s.

Gull hawking can be practised at any time of the year. However, because the smaller gulls, the common gull and the black-headed gull are protected species, you will need a quarry licence from the Department of the Environment, thus restricting your hawking to the winter months. St Quintin flew gulls from October through to February or March. Blaine, who combined his gull hawking with his grouse hawking in Scotland, only flew gulls from August through to October or November, but he found that immature gulls did not usually provide worthwhile flights in the early part of the season.

Several species of gull are now common in many parts of the country, making them a readily-available quarry. Herring gulls and immature greater and lesser black-backed gulls are often found around rubbish tips and dumps or following farm machinery working a field. These larger gulls are more easily caught then the smaller species as they cannot shift from the stoop in the same way. Nevertheless, once on the ground they can give a tiercel quite a buffeting. Immature gulls are normally more easily caught then the adults. The most difficult but rewarding flights are at common gulls or the very active and buoyant black-headed gulls.

Gulls can be flown at in country far more enclosed than is required for proper rook hawking. However, gulls will 'put-in' to open water, lakes, lochs and large rivers, so land near to the sea or any estuary should be avoided. Fortunately, gulls now spend much of their time inland and there are few areas of Britain where gull hawking could not be attempted. The flight can usually be followed on foot, since it is only in very rough weather that it is likely to cover many miles.

Hawks suitable for gull hawking

Both falcon and tiercel peregrines can be flown at gulls, and results show that eyasses have proved as successful at this difficult quarry as their wild-caught brothers. Sakers and sakrets might well prove ideal for this very aerial flight, and the largest gulls could provide a worthy opponent for the gyrfalcon. Both peregrines and sakers have taken seagulls when out rook hawking and there should be little difficulty in entering them to this quarry. Immature gulls allow a much closer approach then the more suspicious rook or crow, so one or two close slips and quick kills should be easy to arrange. Gyrs might prove rather more difficult to enter to gulls; one or two eyasses have been tried but showed little enthusiasm for the flight. However, a passage gyrfalcon which was also tried, took to gulls from the start, seemingly knowing all about them.

Hawks will eat gull flesh and some even seem to enjoy it. However, if a hawk shows any signs of distate then feed some warm pigeon or quail meat up through the wing of the gull as the falcon sits on her kill. She will hopefully be fooled into thinking that a gull is not so bad to eat after all. St Quintin was of the opinion that his tiercels did not care for seagull as a diet, and he found it necessary to give them washed meat on occasion (that is meat soaked in water overnight to reduce its goodness), to make them eager for blood.

Flying a cast of hawks at seagulls

As seagulls are normally flown with a cast of hawks, it is important to get the two hawks accustomed to feeding and flying together. Even sitting next to one another on the screen perch helps and later in their training they can be called to the lure at the same time. A larger than usual lure can be used, although I find it easier to use two small lures which can be thrown out together or separately as one wishes. Mavrogordato had a lure at either end of his lure line, so that while he held the one lure in his hand he swung the other until the hawks were almost up when he dropped both lures to the ground.

Seagulls have an untiring, buoyant flight and only the best of hawks, fit, strong and in top condition, will be capable of taking the smaller gulls throughout the season. In fact St Quintin considered it almost impossible for a single hawk to kill a common or black-headed gull within several miles unless it was done at the first stoop. If hawks were lost he blamed it on the fact that the cast of hawks divided if flown at a large flock, thus taking on separate gulls and killing them a great distance away. This clearly illustrates the importance of careful and accurate slipping of the second hawk in order to minimise the chances of them dividing. It is better to slip the second hawk after the lead hawk has separated the chosen gull from its companions and has brought it down close to the ground with a well-timed stoop. Unlike rooks, gulls are not easy to separate and the lead hawk may need to make two or three accurate stoops to single out his chosen bird. The second hawk will be more inclined to join in the pursuit of a gull which is clearly under pressure from the lead hawk. Occasionally, although both hawks initially start at separate gulls, one of the hawks, having perhaps lost his chosen gull, will see the gull being pursued at some disadvantage by his partner below him and will turn and join in that flight. A cast of hawks working together is a pretty sight as each in turn makes his stoop while the other swings up to once more gain height over the gull and so discourage it from ringing away into the clouds. Stoop after stoop will follow until the gull is forced down near the ground and, in evading the stoop of one hawk, twists into the path of the partner and is taken.

A cast of good tiercels flown at a black-headed gull must surely rank as the finest 'out of the hood' flight left in Great Britain. Gullhawking is a very acceptable substitute for the noble flights at heron and kite so popular in times gone past.

Barbary falcon on magpie

Magpies

In the past a cast of tiercels was also considered to be the ideal combination for the exciting flight at the lowly magpie. Magpies might be thought to be slow and unenterprising quarry but in practice, flown in the right country, they provide a testing and interesting flight in which the field play an active part. Once again the country needs to be open and free of woods, spinneys, tall hedgerow trees or large farm buildings. However, scrub, small clumps of bushes, thorn trees or skimpy hedges are almost a necessity, and play a major part in making a flight possible. If the country is very open there is some risk that the magpie will clear off to safer horizons on the appearance of the hawking party. With some available cover the magpie will feel confident enough to stay put.

For a long time the 'home' of magpie hawking was Ireland, and many members of the Old Hawking Club enjoyed excellent sport in the counties of Cork, Kildare and Tipperary. Magpies also provided the occasional flight on Salisbury Plain when members of the Old Hawking Club went there for their spring rook hawking.

Although traditionally a cast of tiercels was used for magpie hawking, falcons and shahins were also used on occasion, and lanners or lannerets might well prove to be perfect for this quarry. The larger hawks are perhaps more likely to fly 'at check' and to set off after rooks in the distance instead of waiting patiently over a thorn bush where 'poor mag' skulks in hiding. More than one strong tiercel has progressed from magpies to rook hawking after 'checking' at rooks and so proving that he was capable of handling the tougher quarry.

Now that the magpie is commonly seen in the countryside there would seem to be little difficulty in finding some in suitable hawking country. However, magpies are secretive birds that rarely travel far from cover, and much searching and spotting with binoculars is needed before a promising slip can be found. Even in country seemingly devoid of any bird life, a walk out into a field might well result in a skulking mag nervously flying up from his feeding on to a convenient bush or fence post from where he can keep an eye on the proceedings.

Slipping at magpies

As with all flights 'out of the hood', the initial slip should be at an upwind magpie. It is better if the falconer can find magpies out in the open, rather than at the edge of cover, so that the lead hawk can at least get in two or three stoops at the selected bird before it reaches the first bushes. A magpie will have quite a struggle to make any headway upwind and so the hawk will bring it down wind to cover, near where the falconer and his supporters are waiting. As the magpie dashes into the bushes the tiercel should wait-on overhead. The best magpie hawks need not wait-on very high, but they should hold a tight umbrella over the skulking magpie, always being in a position to stoop as soon as the mag is dislodged from cover.

If there are lots of magpies there is some risk of a keen hawk seeing the others as he waits-on and chasing away after them, so the sooner the field can eject the hunted magpie the better. The longer the magpie is in cover the more time it has to recover both its wind and its composure, and the more the waiting hawk has to work to keep its position over the bush. The falconer has the second hawk ready on his fist, and as soon as the magpie breaks cover and the lead hawk stoops, then he slips the second hawk. Next both hawks stoop in turn or wait-on while the energetic field rushes up to once again re-flush the clever mag. Finally, one of the hawks makes a rush at the magpie and grabs it just as it is about to either drop into a bush or attempt to land and dodge the hawks on the ground.

Magpies can be hawked at any time of the year but the autumn is most convenient because at that time there are young, inexperienced magpies (recognisable by their shorter tails) in the family groups, and these are more easily caught, making them good quarry for entering hawks. Beware of very hot, still weather at the start of the season since a hot hawk waiting-on for the umpteenth time will be tempted to go on the soar. A hard-pressed magpie is not easily persuaded to leave the safety of even the thinnest cover. The crack of a hunting whip is the most effective way to encourage the mag to leave but you might also find a starting pistol useful. Just as the beak or feet of the rook have long been the trophy for the rook hawker, so too is the long tail of the defeated magpie cherished, and it looks very striking cockaded in the falconer's hat.

Most hawks will learn quickly to wait-on over 'put-in' quarry, particularly if they are always served when the quarry is re-flushed. Remember this and if the magpie should get into cover from which you are unlikely to be able to shift it within a reasonable time, take your hawks down to the lure. Failure to do this will soon encourage the hawks to take stand, sitting down rather than waiting-on as they should, and much of the beauty of the magpie flight will be lost. A tiercel which is slow to learn to wait-on for game will often benefit from a season flown at magpies. If flown with an experienced hawk to wait-on over the put-in magpies, the tiercel will learn by example and may well turn into a first-rate partridge hawk.

Surprisingly, few falconers have practised seagull or magpie hawking in recent years even though these two flights perhaps offer the best opportunities to enjoy quality hawking at readily-available quarry.

5
Hawking dogs

One of the great pleasures of game hawking is the additional enjoyment of using a good working dog in an understanding partnership with your hawk. Certain species of game can be spotted by eye and flown at with a hawk with little or no help from a spaniel or 'bird' dog, but much of the pleasure and uncertainty of game hawking is then lacking. One of the elements of game hawking that helps to make it a sporting flight is the uncertainty of not knowing whether the dog is pointing game; perhaps the grouse have already flown or they are a long way upwind of the point. One senior falconer has often been heard to complain that his pointers and setters are a 'necessary evil'. Thus while there are moments in every game falconer's life when he thinks his dogs are evil, he also recognises that they are necessary, especially for grouse hawking but also for partridge and pheasant hawking.

Breeds of dog

Blaine, Lascelles and Fisher all claim that it is on record that English setters are better suited to the specialised work involved in hawking than other breeds of 'bird' dog such as pointers and Irish or Gordon setters. However, both Blaine and Fisher hawked over pointers as well as setters and certainly found them equal to the work.

'Old Mac' on point

Hawking dogs

Today, nearly all grouse hawks are flown over English pointers, with the occasional support of an English setter, Irish setter or German pointer. It really is a matter of personal preference as to which breed of 'bird' dog is used; there are good and bad strains and specimens in all of the breeds. Nevertheless, at the present time there is certainly a far greater availability of good working pointers than of any other breed. When choosing a dog it is worth remembering that, while you work the dog for a matter of three or four months each year, you have to look at him and live with him all the year round. Certainly, although the ability of the dog in the field should be the first consideration, a good-looking animal is easier to live with.

You will need a confident, wide-ranging dog for grouse hawking on all but the most heavily stocked of moors. The dog should be tireless in his work and staunch without being 'sticky' on point. He should ideally only point grouse, leaving ground game strictly alone. In recent years many pointers have nearly, if not quite, fulfilled all that was demanded of them, and along with the English setter they should be regarded as the ideal for grouse hawking. Although they are often considered unruly, if chosen from the best working strains the Red or Irish setter is also an excellent working dog. Unfortunately, however, their wonderful rich colour is somewhat against them when it comes to hawking on a grouse moor. This is because they are not easy to see against the heathery background, making it difficult for both hawk and falconer to find them when they are on point some distance away or in deep heather. If a hawk is regularly flown over an Irish setter she will soon learn to recognise the dog, but a hawk that is normally flown over an English pointer or setter might well not recognise easily that the Irish setter is performing the same duty. Gordon setters are also a difficult colour to find easily on the hill, but pointers and English setters, dogs that usually show a lot of white in their coat do not suffer from the same disadvantage. So, it is best to choose a puppy that will show up well on the moor.

The various European pointer/retriever breeds all have a dedicated following of enthusiasts who argue that their particular favourite is undoubtedly the ideal dog for the falconer. Unfortunately, like the Irish and Gordon setters, all these breeds are unsuitable in colour as well as being generally neither fast enough nor sufficiently wide-ranging to satisfy any grouse falconers other than their enthusiastic owners. The fact that they also retrieve (just as many English pointers and setters do with little or no encouragement) is of little benefit to the grouse falconer because, except when a grouse is knocked down into a loch or river, it is better that the grouse is re-flushed rather than retrieved so that the hawk may catch it as it should.

The pointer/retriever breeds are just as well suited to partridge and pheasant hawking as the pointer or the setter, and the Brittany spaniel, which points and hunts cover as well as any breed, could well prove the ideal dog for the purpose.

Dogs suitable for grouse hawking

A dog is required to quarter a wide stretch of country for grouse hawking. He should work the country chosen by the falconer and not that which he prefers to hunt. Once he is experienced, the dog should work up, down or across wind with equal enthusiasm. Although the dog should quarter and turn at the end of his beat without instruction, adjusting his range to the terrain and conditions, he should be obedient to the turn whistle, so that if necessary he can be 'handled' on to ground that the falconer wants him to investigate.

Although the dog may well find the grouse at a great range, with experience he should understand how close he can draw up to the grouse without fear of flushing them. A dog that points his grouse at close range without accidentally flushing them, is not necessarily 'short nosed'; he may well have found the grouse some long way off. With a dog that is consistently close to his birds, the falconer will have less problem in deciding how far upwind he will need to walk beyond the dog to 'head the point' and thus ensure that the grouse will flush down wind. Of course scent varies with different conditions and wind strength and this must be taken into account when heading the point. On scenting grouse 'Quill', an old pointer of mine, would hold point at some distance away from them, usually standing tall on point. Once the falcon had circled a few times over the grouse, 'Quill' would rush in and then 'drop' on point very close to the hidden grouse so that he was ready to flush at a moment's notice. He clearly understood the risk of getting too close to his birds before the silhouette of the mounting falcon had pinned them down.

The hawking dog should hold his point for as long as necessary so that the falconer can get his hawk into her correct position and at her best pitch. However, the dog should not be 'sticky' on point, refusing to move to flush the grouse. A 'sticky' dog can easily lose his grouse when on point because the birds may well creep away, perhaps across the wind, and unless the dog keeps up with them they will not be in front of him when they should be. A dog that draws slowly after running grouse tends to drive them before him. A better dog will dash upwind or make a sharp, sudden cast across the wind, holding the grouse by these sudden movements.

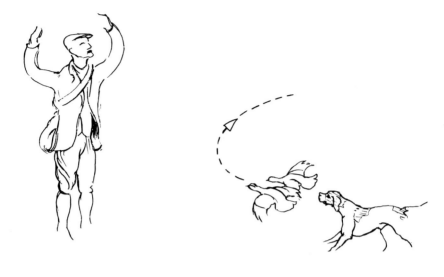

Fig. 116 Here the pointer flushes to order and the grouse are turned downwind by the presence of the falconer and the hawk, upwind

Flushing game

If the dog will not flush to order, then the falconer will be forced either to walk in with him or to attempt to flush the grouse himself by walking down wind directly towards his dog. Either option will almost certainly result in an upwind flush which will spoil the flight. If the falconer has some assistants he could send one in to walk the grouse up with the pointer or to flush them with a spaniel, while he does his best to keep the falcon well upwind of the point. Thus the grouse will turn down wind past the assistant rather than face having to fly under the waiting hawk, but it is far better if the pointer or setter will flush to order.

As Blaine wrote, 'A setter that can be trained to dash in, and flush the nearest bird of a brood, dropping instantly to wing, is invaluable, but such dogs are few and far between.' 'Ranger' and 'Free', two of Blaine's best setters, did this to perfection. Fortunately for today's falconers, who can rarely afford the luxury of a dog handler, many of the dogs used at the present time will flush to order. However, few of them drop to wing, and it is here that many falconer's dogs are at fault. If your dog drops to wing, that is he lays down as soon as grouse flush from his point, then he is under control. This means that at the crucial moment all attention can be focused on the stooping hawk rather than the dog. A covey of grouse is often well spread in front of the point, and if your dog drops to wing there is every chance that two, three or even four flights might follow

Fig. 117 Grouse breaking upwind as the falconer attempts to flush game himself

from the same covey. Should your hawk fail to kill then there is every chance that you can serve her again when she returns to you.

Few dogs will regularly find you more than one point from a covey, because in their enthusiasm they will flush the whole brood or family in a single rush. However, if the dog then drops to wing at least he is under control and ready to help you should you need him to find a put-in bird or a fresh grouse. A dog that does not drop to wing will very soon start to chase after the grouse and the hawk until everything gets out of control, with the dog rushing about flushing put-in grouse to right and left, completely oblivious of both hawk and falconer. If your dog drops to wing you can enjoy your falcon's stoop unhindered by worries about what the dog is doing. Should your falcon kill her grouse, then go to the dog and reward him for his help but keep him dropped so that he understands how important that is and it becomes a confirmed habit. This is the time to make a fuss of your dog – not when it has raced down to the kill as madly as the falconer probably has, so that you in fact reward him for doing something wrong.

Although all 'bird' dogs seem to thoroughly enjoy being out with the hawks, you should never forget what an important part they play in bringing about a successful flight, and you should make a fuss of them when they have done all that you asked of them. All too often dogs are overworked and unfairly blamed for whatever goes wrong. Remember that they are only dogs and they do make mistakes.

Dog leads

A simple rope or nylon slip lead that can be tucked into a pocket easily is useful for leading a spare dog that is not working, or to encourage a tired dog to take a rest. A dog should be taught not to pull on the lead as this is exhausting both to the dog and to the person who is unfortunate enough to have to lead it. The dog should also be trained to walk to heel. Contrary to the belief of many field trial enthusiasts, walking to heel

Fig. 118 A selection of dog leads and couples

does not deter a properly trained dog from doing his work with enthusiasm and drive. Pointers such as 'Queenie', 'Pixie', 'Snipe' and 'Daffy' have all walked to heel (though on occasion requiring a gentle reminder!), and yet have proved their worth both in the field and at trials.

Many 'bird' dogs find falconry and falconers very exciting, even overstimulating, and they might well benefit from a season or two working with guns before progressing to the more exacting and demanding task of working with hawks. A successful field trial dog does not necessarily make a good hawking dog, however stylish and bold he is in his work. Too many trial dogs are overhandled, with a whistle being blown at every turn or point. A hawking dog should work equally well with or without the whistle, and should rely on his own initiative while still remaining obedient to the whistle. One whistle should be sufficient since the dog only needs to respond to the signals for 'drop', 'turn' and 'come'. More whistles only add to the confusion, particularly if a Thunderer whistle is used for the hawk.

If your falcon puts grouse into cover at a reasonable distance then it is well worth while letting the dog find and point them so that the falcon can once again be served. Put-in grouse will sometimes run a great distance, and there is no doubt that hunting them out will encourage your pointer to track ground scent, that is to follow the line of the running grouse with his nose to ground. When ranging, a 'bird' dog normally locates grouse by air scent, and he should gallop with his head held high. There is some risk involved in this in that too much work on ground scent might spoil the head carriage of a dog. Nevertheless, the dogs definitely enjoy the excitement of hunting a grouse out of a ditch or burn, and both dog and hawk soon learn to co-operate in bringing the hunt to a successful conclusion.

Dogs suitable for partridge and pheasants

Most of what has gone before in this chapter will also be relevant if the quarry is partridge or pheasants. However, as will be seen in the chapter on game hawking, the quarry may be spotted initially by the falconer, so that the hawk is flown before the dog is run. These days, when little stubble is left in the corn fields after harvest, there is less suitable 'dogging' ground available, although partridge and pheasants can be 'dogged' in root fields, low game cover or on early winter corn.

Partridge do not seem to 'carry' as much scent as grouse, and a dog who has previously only worked on the moors may take a little time to adjust to the different quarry and the new field conditions. When pheasants are in cover such as kale, it is better to beat out the field with a line of falconers and a spaniel or two; a pointing dog is often difficult to spot in such tall cover and the pheasants will invariably run ahead of the dog, making them difficult to flush.

6

Game hawking

In his book called *Falconry* (Allen, 1936) Colonel Gilbert Blaine wrote that: 'Game hawking is the most difficult branch of the falconer's art, as it is also the most artificial. In all other forms of falconry the falcon is flown straight 'out of the hood' at her quarry.'

Gilbert Blaine grouse hawking with 'Lady Jane' in 1922

Unlike any other flight, the game hawk is flown *before* the quarry is flushed. No doubt grouse, and in particular partridge, could be caught by a good hawk flown 'out of the hood', but the long chase would often take the hawk out of sight and little would be seen of the flight. With the hawk waiting-on and the game being flushed by dog and falconer below, the dramatic stoop of a falcon can be enjoyed at close quarters. Furthermore, the falcon will very often kill, cutting the quarry down in a cloud of feathers at the very feet of the spectators.

Game hawk leaving the fist

Game hawking requires careful co-operation between the dog, the falconer and the hawk. The falcon must be encouraged to wait-on, patiently circling overhead, the dog must honestly point the hidden game, and both the dog and the falconer must then flush at the right moment so that the falcon has the opportunity to make a telling stoop. Provided all goes according to plan, game hawking is one of the most dramatic sights in the sporting world, but if the co-operation does not exist then no sport can prove more disappointing. As Stanley Allen once noted, 'There is no sport better than good falconry and nothing worse than the bad version.'

In game hawking the hawk is normally flown as soon as the dog is pointing game, or game has been spotted. The falcon is given time to mount and to fly higher and higher until she is 'waiting-on', circling over the dog or the falconer. When the falcon is as high as she will go the game is flushed down wind. The falcon turns over and drives earthwards, falling at a great pace, before rapidly closing with the fleeing game and cutting one of them over in a puff of feathers. Fortunately 'waiting-on' comes naturally, at least to most peregrines, but encouragement must still be given by always serving the falcons with quarry when they are overhead. Nothing succeeds like success and repeated success at game from a position over dog or falconer will condition the hawk to wait-on in expectation of game being accurately flushed underneath her.

After training, the sooner a hawk is introduced to her intended quarry the better, and so the fact that the grouse season starts as early as 12 August in Great Britain ensures perfect timing for entering a hacked eyas.

Grouse hawking country

For grouse hawking the best country is open moorland, with few trees and crofts and not too many hills. The flat bog moors of Caithness and parts of Sutherland are ideal, and have long been the choice of many falconers over the years. The moor should not be too broken up with burns or drainage ditches and lochs, particularly if these have islands in

Falconers and keepers on the grouse moors in 1897

them; more than one hapless falconer has had to strip off and swim out through the cold Highland water to an island to recover hawk and grouse. Being out of the reach of deer and sheep, most islands are covered profusely in heather and scrub, and so prove an irresistable lure to a hard-pressed grouse.

Hawking on the grouse moors

The moor should be well stocked with grouse, but it need not hold the numbers found on the top 'driving' moors of Angus or Perthshire. Certainly, if falconers are paying the not inconsiderable rents demanded today for grouse moors, they should at least be able to expect to find a dozen or so points in an afternoon without having to walk right across the county in so doing. Many of the finest grouse moors in the North have now been swallowed up by the ever-encroaching forestry, which not only destroys that moor for ever but also damages all the neighbouring grouse ground. I find it extraordinary that grouse moor owners do not seem to care when huge drainage ditches flood on to their land, turning into bog what might be good grouse-breeding ground. Grouse moors further south, with their gently rolling hills, are also suitable for hawking and, being heather moors, will usually carry a bigger stock of grouse. A great glen or valley with hills all around can be used in any wind conditions.

In choosing a moor, do enquire about the prevailing winds in the area because you might find it difficult to fly hawks on what seems to be a lovely moor if most of the ground slopes away from the prevailing wind. Very mountainous ground should be avoided if possible; hawks are all too easily lost when chasing grouse out of sight in very broken ground, and while they might well be found with telemetry, hawking all day with a telemetry receiver in one hand is not my idea of game hawking. Hawks fly high with very little effort in mountainous country, floating up on thermals or strong hill winds to ridge-soar over dog and falconer. Although this is very often exciting, with the hawk reaching a great height, it doesn't give the same satisfaction as seeing the hawk working her own way upwards to eventually wait-on correctly positioned to stoop at the grouse.

The cost of grouse moors

The grouse falconer is at some disadvantage in seeking a suitable moor for his sport. Unless the falconer has the opportunity to continue flying his hawks at partridge or pheasants on returning south, he needs to rent a moor for an absolute minimum of four or five weeks. Shooting parties are often satisfied with one or two afternoons on the moors and in that time they may well shoot as many grouse as the falconer will take during the whole season. However, if the falconer is renting the moor and his living accommodation by the week, he will find his grouse very expensive.

Waiting-on

Very little can be done to encourage a hawk to wait-on until the season opens. By all means call her to the lure, but do not stoop a young hack hawk at the swung lure. It is better to call her from your assistant and, when she has nearly reached you, to hide the lure momentarily so that she 'throws up' (swings up over you due to the impetus of the flight) to wait over you. Next, you immediately throw out the lure down wind. Take your hawk to a gently sloping hillside on the moor, with the wind blowing up the face of the hill. Holding the lure in your right hand so that she may see it, let the hawk fly. She will almost certainly circle, watching for the lure to be thrown out, and with some small help from the wind she may gain a little height. Do not try her too long, but when she is upwind of you throw out the lure down wind and reward her well. Do no fly her more than once and let her take the greater part of her daily ration from the lure.

It is also a good plan to take your hawking dog with you when flying the hawk to the lure. Drop the dog as if on point and then throw out the lure. Let the dog come up to the hawk while she is on the lure so that she becomes thoroughly accustomed to him. Passage and haggard hawks are much more likely to be nervous of a dog, perhaps associating it with a fox or wolf which they may have come across when in the wild. Two or three days at the most is sufficient at the lure. The day before entering to grouse it is useful to use a dead grouse as the lure and to let the hawk eat at least some of her meal from the pelt. With your older hawks there is no need to do any lure flying, because should they know the game they will, if flown in a reasonable place, immediately go up and wait-on (although perhaps not as high or for so long as they would when fit).

When first trying a passage or a haggard at game, particularly if she has previously been flown 'out of the hood' at quarry, hold her attention by keeping your lure, or better still a dead grouse, in your spare hand. If she begins to wander too far, attract her attention by flapping the lure or dead grouse just enough to turn her towards you. Then flush the grouse so that she sees that it is you and your dog who produce potential quarry for her. Most passage hawks or haggards learn very quickly, and though not every wild-caught hawk turns out to be a high waiting-on game hawk, they quickly learn the part played by dog and falconer.

The first flight at quarry

When the great day arrives to give your young hawk her first chance at quarry, fly her late in the day so that she will have rather more edge to her appetite. Hopefully, she will be ready to enter early in the season, and if a covey of young grouse can be found she will have every chance of success at her first venture. Again, as when flying her to the lure, if possible fly her on a gently sloping hillside so that it will be easy for her to gain a little height over you. Choose a point that is in open country, well away from bracken or a burn in which the grouse could seek early refuge. Use your most reliable dog and take every possible care to weigh the balance in favour of the hawk. Go right up to the dog before slipping

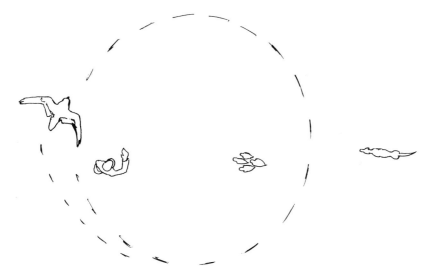

Fig. 119 The best time to flush game is just as the hawk turns

your hawk so that little time is lost in flushing the grouse. The falcon will have her attention on you rather than the dog at this stage in her training, and so it is important that you should be close to the grouse when they flush. If successful, within a few days your hawk will begin to watch the dog in expectation of grouse being flushed.

Watch your young hawk carefully. As long as she continues to mount, let her, but as soon as she starts to glide rather than beat her wings, particularly as she comes forward into the wind when circling, then as quickly as possible flush the grouse down wind while the falcon is upwind of where you expect the grouse to be hiding. Later, when your hawk goes higher, it is not so critical to flush at the exact moment that your hawk turns.

No self-respecting hawk will ignore grouse that rise right underneath her, and if she chooses a young grouse from the covey she may kill at her first attempt. Luck, of course, plays its part in these early flights. A captive-bred, unhacked tiercel of mine was shown grouse on his very first flight off the creance. As we walked out on to the moor, I was just about to call the tiercel to the lure when the dog came on point. So although the tiercel had not gained any height he started chasing a single old grouse that rose from the point. He chased that grouse right across the moor before finally losing it in the burn. Then he turned and came back across the sky before I had the lure out, getting higher and higher as he came. I was just about to attempt to lure him down when luckily I noticed that the dog was still on point. By now the tiercel was high over us, so I jumped in and up got a whole covey of young grouse. Down came the tiercel and scooped up a little grouse like a professional. He was to become a very fine tiercel.

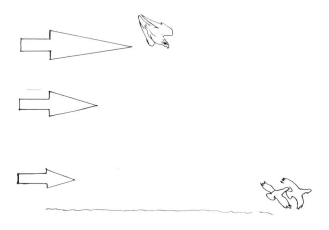

Fig. 120 Increasing wind strength at height assists the hawk in stooping down wind

The importance of flushing down wind

No falconer who has ever had the pleasure of flying high, waiting-on game hawks would ever question the oft written advice that all game should be flushed down wind. Any one who has studied the wind and its ways knows that the wind strength increases the higher you are above the ground, and a falcon waiting-on at say 600ft (180m) is facing a very much stronger wind than the grouse would encounter a few feet above the ground. Of course if your hawks do not wait-on then it is of little consequence in which direction you flush game. One only has to see a hawk stooping upwind to see how much 'punch' is taken out of his stoop. Grouse, like all game birds who have rapid wing beat on small wings, cut into a head wind with little trouble, and on a windy day they whistle down the wind at an alarming speed. Just watch a hawk coming down from a really high pitch at down wind grouse, and listen to the 'blow' as she tips a grouse head over heels into the heather. You will have no doubt that the advice so often given by Blaine, Fisher, Stevens and Frank, that game should always be flushed down wind, is right if you wish to witness the headlong stoop of a falcon at its very finest.

Of course, if you are flying a game hawk in mountainous country where she will have to be flown on the windward side of a hill, it will be difficult to flush the grouse down wind, that is uphill, and therefore it is better to flush them along the hillside. But if the grouse are found on the flat, well out from the hillside, then they can be flushed down wind as usual. The hawk can, and will, make use of the hillside to gain height.

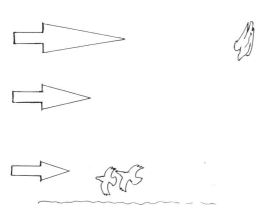

Fig. 121 Increasing wind strength is a handicap to a hawk stooping upwind

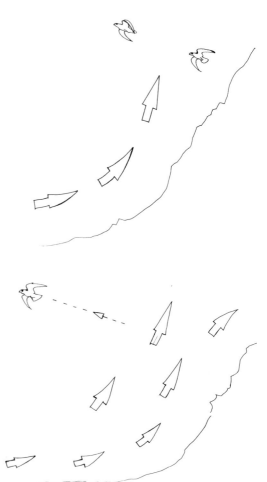

Fig. 122 This hawk is assisted by wind-lift on a steep hillside

Fig. 123 A hawk coming forward to wait-on over the pointer after gaining height on a windward hillside

Waiting-on in hilly country

Although I believe that great hillsides can spoil a game hawk and make her lazy, gently sloping hillsides can be a great help in teaching hawks to wait-on, because the natural lift of the wind will make it much easier for an inexperienced hawk to mount over the dog. However, if a hawk is always flown with the advantage of hill-lift she will come to depend on it, and will go a great distance away from the point in search of a helpful hill. While she is gone, the grouse will more than likely take advantage of her absence and fly off when she is furthest away. A game hawk should ideally mount over the dog, so that at all times she commands any grouse below her.

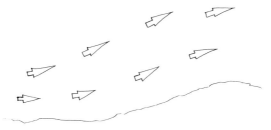

Fig. 124 On a gently sloping hill maximum lift is part way up the hillside

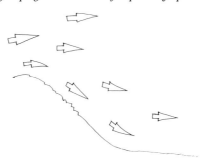

Fig. 125 Wind will be of no assistance to a hawk waiting-on on the lea of a hill

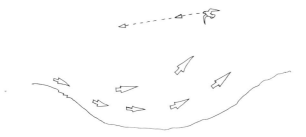

Fig. 126 A hawk finding lift on a hill, then coming forward towards a pointer on the lea of the slope opposite

All too often, particularly in windy weather, grouse are only to be found sheltering on the lee side of a hill. Indeed, if grouse are scarce it is only in such sheltered places that you may enjoy any sport. An experienced hawk will often search for some wind lift or dead air in which she can make height. Then, when she has reached her pitch, she will slide across the sky to wait-on as she should over the patient pointer. If she is high enough she may well find lift in the wind wave rolling up the face of the hill on which the grouse have been found. As noted above, there is some risk of the grouse slipping away when the hawk is not over them.

Correct serving of quarry

There is no better way to teach a hawk to wait-on than to repeatedly serve her with her proper quarry, that is the wild quarry that you want her to hunt. An experienced dog that will run in and flush the game he has been pointing on command, is a great help. With such a dog the game can be flushed at the exact moment when the hawk is correctly positioned to stoop at the grouse. However, with such clever pointers there is a danger that the falconer will spoil a potentially good hawk if he continues to flush grouse, with great accuracy, right into the 'feet' of the hawk. Of course the falconer does want his hawk to catch grouse, but it is also important that they should be caught in style. If the falcon is allowed to believe that she only has to sweep about the sky, knowing that the dog and the falconer will flush the grouse when she momentarily sweeps up over the point, then she will never become a proper game hawk.

All too often the complaint is heard that the dog flushed them all wrong. What is really at fault is that the hawk neither waits-on high enough nor long enough. By all means give your falcon every possible help on her first few essays at grouse. With luck, it will be a covey in front of the point rather than a single old grouse, and the hawk will soon begin to realise that it is when she is over the dog and has the advantage of height that she has her best chance of catching a grouse. It is extraordinary how often one hawk will appear to have all of the luck, with perfect flushes at young grouse in ideal terrain, whereas another hawk will repeatedly be out of luck, with false points or tough old single grouse that are virtually uncatchable.

Positioning

As the falcon begins to understand what is required of her, allow her more and more time to mount to her proper pitch. Sometimes a hawk will mount to a certain height then, resting on her wings, gives the impression that she will go no higher. Give her a little more time and, seeing that you are not moving in to flush the grouse, she will often go yet higher. After a number of kills your hawk should understand what is required of her. While going higher, a hawk will occasionally start to drift from her position so that instead of patrolling in her correct place, just upwind of the pointing dog, she will drift down wind in her circling. Should she do so, flush the grouse while she is furthest away from you. She will almost certainly be beaten to cover upwind, but a lesson will have been learned.

One of my young tiercels started by doing just this. He was a very high mounting tiercel, but after about ten kills in his first season he had become a little independent. Thus even when he was at a great pitch he would drift away from the frantic falconer and the patient pointer. Not wanting to miss the chance of a kill I would rush about trying everything to encourage him to come over the point. One day, flying on Camster moor as a guest of Christian Saar, the tiercel drifted further and further from the point. After watching the extraordinary performance of the falconer for some time, Christian walked over and, in his quiet way, advised me to flush the grouse when the tiercel was furthest away. As Christian put it 'Do you just want to kill a grouse or do you want a top-class game hawk?' We flushed the grouse and although the tiercel did his best he was beaten to a large block of forestry. He was 'taught a lesson' on a further two occasions and soon learned to know his proper place.

Ideally, all should be quiet as your hawk mounts over you. However, even the quietest of falconers cannot resist flapping his glove, a handkerchief or a pigeon wing as he walks or runs around to head the point. If you must flap something (I can't resist flapping my glove however hard I try not to), do not show your lure at this moment unless the hawk is leaving the scene of operations; the lure should be kept for luring her down and then rewarding her. Even if your falcon is drifting away, it is better to use a dead grouse to get her attention. Other falconers just cannot keep quiet and shout, whistle, 'Brrr, brrr' to their hawks or even quietly call 'Hup, hup' to encourage them to mount higher. If the hawk is accustomed to this she will certainly react to the call and go higher and higher as the falconer closes with the pointing dog.

The best dogs will flush to order, but this can sometimes spoil a flight as the hawk quickly learns to recognise the instruction to the dog to 'put 'em up' and will start to stoop before the grouse are flushed. On occasion I have seen a falcon stoop right down to ground level without there being a grouse in sight, either because the dog has falsely pointed or because it has missed the exact position of the grouse in rushing in to them. A change in the routine, such as using a spaniel to flush or even walking in and flushing the grouse yourself, might help to cure such behaviour. When doing this there is every likelihood of the grouse breaking away upwind. To reduce the risk of this happening, only move forward when the hawk is well upwind of the point.

Waiting-on over the dog

The very best hawks soon learn to wait-on over the pointer rather than the falconer, and to position themselves slightly upwind of the dog, according to the strength of the wind. With the falcon upwind of the expected grouse, there is every possibility of the grouse flushing down wind rather than facing the risk of passing directly under the waiting falcon. The stronger the wind, the further upwind of the dog the grouse are likely to be hidden, and the clever hawk will learn this and adjust her position according to the conditions.

Once a hawk has learned that it is the dog that finds the grouse then, even if the grouse are wild and difficult to approach, the hawk can be slipped at some distance from the point. On seeing the dog, the hawk will fly towards him, making height as she goes. Once she has arrived over the dog the grouse will be pinned down by her easily recognisable outline in the sky, and the falconer can then make his way to the point. The higher the hawk is, the less exact you need to be about flushing the grouse. However, the higher and further upwind the hawk is, the better down wind stoop she will achieve.

Of course a hawk that is very high can command grouse rising a good deal wide of the point, but because she will take so long coming down to her grouse, they may well have dropped into convenient cover before she reaches them. The hawk does not often have the opportunity to stoop straight into her grouse because they normally fly only a few feet, often only a few inches, above the heather when flushed under a hawk (partridge and pheasants usually fly higher). If a hawk stoops straight into her chosen bird she may well have difficulty in evading the ground. Inexperienced hawks occasionally attempt to hit a grouse in this way, and I have known two tiercels to knock themselves out, bouncing on the heather in one direction while their grouse bounced in the other. In both cases the grouse got up and went away rejoicing. A grouse hawk normally needs to flatten out from his stoop behind his quarry. He can then either rush up to the grouse and tip it over in a cloud of feathers or neatly 'bind-to' his quarry (that is catch hold of it), to land in the heather still holding on to the grouse.

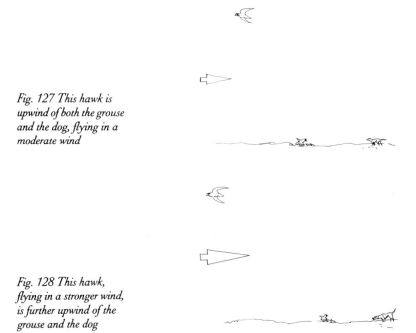

Fig. 127 This hawk is upwind of both the grouse and the dog, flying in a moderate wind

Fig. 128 This hawk, flying in a stronger wind, is further upwind of the grouse and the dog

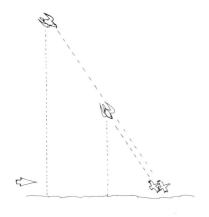

Fig. 129 (left) A hawk waiting-on at great height can afford to be further upwind of the grouse

Fig. 130 (below, left) The higher the falcon soars the more ground is covered

Fig. 131 (below, right) The end of a stoop with the grouse well above the ground

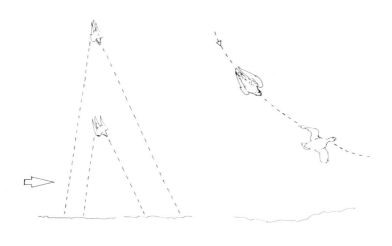

Fig. 132 The end of a stoop with the grouse close to the ground

The kill

Because the grouse is so often hit from behind by inexperienced hawks (and some hawks never greatly improve), the blow does little more than encourage the grouse to reach a greater speed or tip it over unharmed in the heather. Although a lot of feathers may be left floating in the air, the grouse will go away again as strong as ever, minus a handful of feathers from the plentiful supply around his tail. The clever hawk (and some seem to know what to do from the very first flight), either strikes the body of the grouse, usually under one wing where the grouse is easily damaged, or aims for its wing, perhaps knocking some of the flight feathers off or breaking a bone. I do not subscribe to the oft-quoted belief that a peregrine can be so accurate in her stoop that she will break the neck of her grouse every time. Although the clever hawk is more likely to do this than the hawk who hits a grouse up the tail end, it is usually more by chance than design. With larger quarry which often cannot shift from a stoop in the same way as a grouse, then hawks can and do consistently take them by the head.

Moulting peregrine tiercel on his first grouse of the season

Although perhaps not so spectacular as when a hawk cuts her quarry over with a well timed blow, binding-to is a sure way of putting another grouse in the pocket. Once firmly held, a grouse rarely gets away. Some hawks are definitely binding-to experts. For example, 'Bitch II', a falcon famous for having taken more grouse in a season than any other hawk in recorded history, preferred to bind-to her quarry and would very often carry it for some way before landing. Thus she had time to turn her head and break the neck of the grouse while still on the wing.

Other hawks seem to prefer to cut over their quarry. Some writers have suggested that hawks usually attempt to bind-to their bird, but if they are flying at a great speed their claws tear through feather and skin and the quarry then falls as if it has been cut over. Of course this can happen, but hawks also undoubtedly cut over their quarry intentionally. Inexperienced hawks occasionally clutch hold of a grouse and land thinking they have their prize, when in fact all they have is a handful of feathers. I remember once seeing an old haggard cutting over a grouse and then turning and landing on the bunch of feathers she had knocked out of the bird while it made its escape.

When flying at grouse or pheasants, tiercels in particular are less likely to bind-to than is the larger falcon. If tiercels manage to clutch large quarry they often slip it just before they hit the ground, as if they know instinctively or have learned by experience that carrying such heavy quarry means they are likely to hit the ground with quite a bump. Although a grouse has excellent footwork on the ground (if it isn't injured), a tiercel is also very quick on its feet and will, if determined enough, almost certainly get a foot on a grouse it has slipped with one or two active pounces.

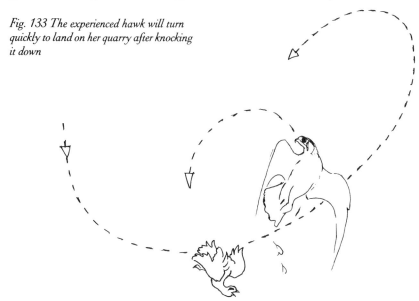

Fig. 133 The experienced hawk will turn quickly to land on her quarry after knocking it down

A grouse knocked down by a hawk is much more likely to dodge the hawk on the ground unless it is killed outright in the stoop. The best hawks turn so quickly from their stoop that they get hold of their grouse before it can hide or take off again. Wild-caught hawks are usually professional in this department, and tiercels are usually very much sharper than falcons. Some eyasses 'throw-up' to a great height from their stoop and will even on occasion take their eye off the grouse and so fail to see it to land on, particularly if they killed it in the stoop.

Grouse in cover

All too often a grouse will drop to the ground just as the hawk comes up to it in its stoop. From there the grouse either immediately jumps to fly upwind or waits until the hawk comes in to try and grab it on the ground. When it is on the ground the grouse waits until the hawk has lost all her speed and has put on the brakes to land, then it springs into the air, leaving the falcon many yards behind it with only the prospect of a long, stern chase to distant cover. The clever hawk will immediately ring up over a 'put-in', rather than try to catch the grouse on the ground, thus giving the falconer and his dog the opportunity to re-find and re-flush the grouse. If the grouse has dropped into thick cover it is easier to get the hawk to mount again, but all too often a cunning old grouse will appear intentionally to show itself only to tempt the hawk to try and catch it on the ground.

When a grouse 'puts-in' to cover within a hundred yards or so of you, by all means go there and, having got your hawk to wait-on again, hunt out the grouse with your dogs. This will teach the falcon both that you are ready to help her and that it is worth the trouble and effort of mounting again and waiting for you to find the grouse. The falcon will benefit from realising that grouse do not always flush immediately and that waiting patiently is more likely to be rewarded than going off. If possible, do not allow the dog to retrieve the grouse; this is easily done if the grouse is tucked in under a peat hag or is hiding in a burn bank. To avoid this, slip a lead on to your dog so that the grouse can be flushed unhindered, if necessary with the toe of your boot. But do keep a good hold on your dog; I once had a brand new boot ruined by my own dog biting at what she thought was a grouse moving under an overhang of heather! Not only was my boot ruined, but also I was lame for many days. Unless it is hit in the stoop there is little point or sport in hunting out 'put-in' grouse, other than for encouraging a young hawk. If grouse are regularly taken by the dog or the hand and are thrown out to the hawk after a 'put-in', your falcon may well give up pressing home her stoop. She will press the grouse just hard enough to force it into cover, knowing that you will kill it for her and that she need not exert herself further. If your hawk 'puts-in' grouse at a distance it is better to leave it and to see if there are more grouse at the original point.

Number of flights

I am more than satisfied if my hawk has waited-on high and well and has killed one grouse in an afternoon. If your hawk fails to kill the first few times she is flown then fly her again, and if she kills reward her well. In her first season there is everything to gain by only flying your hawk once each day. If she kills or returns well to the lure, feed her up. Even though she is flying at much the same weight as she would be when in the moult, she will improve in her performance and also remain obedient to the lure. Does it really matter very much to a sportsman whether his hawk catches twenty or forty grouse in her first season? It is more satisfying to have a high mounting, obedient and confident hawk which will serve him well for many seasons. In most cases it is better to leave a healthy population of grouse to breed and provide sport for the following season, whether this is for you or for others to enjoy. When grouse are numerous, then you should be grateful to the gods of the moors since you can then fly your old hawks two or three times a day.

Hawking weather

A clear blue sky with a warm, moderate wind is perfect weather for game hawking, and few hawks will not go up in such conditions. However, the moors of the North are often battered by gale force winds. Except when there are extreme weather conditions, there is no reason why your hawk should not be flown at grouse. Experienced hawks will often go very high in wild, windy weather, and flights can be very dramatic even if the number of grouse in the game larder at the end of the day is not as large as one might have hoped. Although grouse are undoubtedly harder to kill in rough weather, a still day after a week of storms should restore the falconer's confidence in his hawk's ability. An inexperienced hawk, or one that is unfit and out of condition, should be flown with care in wild weather, and discretion might be wiser than valour. It is better to keep a hawk for another day than to see her whistle down the wind, never to be seen again. However, if conditions are reasonable you should fly her because the next day may be even worse, the exercise will do her good and, provided that she is served with quarry, little harm can be done.

Flying hawks in rain

Most game hawks fly particularly well in light rain and will wait-on successfully even when wet. Heavy rain soon waterlogs and discourages the hawks, but not their ever-hopeful and enthusiastic masters. Although nobody enjoys being labelled a 'fair-weather falconer', I am always willing to call it a day after going to the hill and being soaked to the skin before a single grouse has been found or a hawk flown. Fog normally puts a stop to operations, but it can roll away at any time, so do not feed up the hawks too early in the day.

Hawking at the end of the grouse season

Grouse hawking is at its very finest later on in the season, when the grouse are strong and confident on the wing and there is a sprinkling of crisp snow on the hill and a bite of frost in the air. After many weeks of flying every day, your hawks are at their best, fit and sure of their ability to catch grouse. They can be fully fed, indeed even gorged each night, and yet they will still be keen to fly because the icy cold nights puts an edge on their appetite. Your hawk should be given plenty of time to mount as high as she can so that she can stoop with ease on any grouse rising underneath her. At the same time the grouse, also very confident, will be less likely to drop ignominiously into the heather. In deep snow some hawks are uncertain about landing on a thrown lure. If possible, it is a good idea to find a wind-blown patch where the snow is thin on the ground. In frosty-snow conditions the hawk bells can easily fill up with snow, and if they freeze they will not ring.

Colonel Blaine was of the opinion that grouse are perhaps easier to kill than partridge for the first fortnight or so of the season, but that after that the greater strength and power of flight the grouse tests the best of hawks. By the middle of September at the latest, grouse are only regularly killed by hawks, whether falcon or tiercel, that wait-on high and accurately, and that are confident in their ability to kill such quarry.

Flying tiercels at grouse

Tiercels can and do kill grouse right through to the end of the season. It is not size and weight that make a hawk successful at grouse, but knowing where to hit the quarry. Some tiercels do need to make two or three stoops at a grouse before they feel confident enough to land on it, but many tiercels kill grouse in the air and continue to do so throughout the season. Colonel Blaine suggested that it was better to give a tiercel a season or two at partridge before flying him at grouse. However, Blaine flew many of his best and most successful tiercels at grouse in their first season.

I have never met a tiercel, either eyas or passager, that would not fly grouse, and I would prefer that they are flown at grouse from the beginning. When brought to Scotland for the first time to fly at grouse after some seasons as a most successful partridge hawk, a lovely tiercel, belonging to a friend was not at all enthusiastic about the larger quarry, and it wasn't until some young grouse were flushed underneath him that he condescended to kill one.

A grouse killed from a low pitch, having hardly enough time to gather its wits or to get into full flight because it is flushed almost into the 'feet' of the stooping hawk, is not very satisfactory and cannot be admired as an example of proper game hawking. From a moderate pitch of 200ft

Although moulting, this tiercel is in perfect plumage and is flying grouse daily

(60m) or so, particularly if the hawk is very exact in its position over the dog, the grouse are likely to drop to the ground as the stooping hawk comes up to them. If the hawk waits-on at 500 or 600ft (150 or 180m) or more, then she will command any grouse that rise to the point. Also, the grouse will seemingly be more willing to keep on the wing, thus promising a better flight.

Soaring versus waiting-on

Some falconers find great pleasure in seeing their hawks way up in the clouds. But while it is true that the stoop will be a dramatic and exciting spectacle from such an extravagant pitch, there is the danger that it will end rather tamely with the grouse reaching cover well before the falcon has a chance to strike at it. Rather than soaring all over the sky and only coming over the point by chance after some twenty minutes, I would prefer that a hawk flies somewhat lower but waits-on correctly and plays her proper part in the art of game hawking. Grouse provide an exciting, testing quarry and are readily available, albeit at an ever-increasing price.

Flying peregrines at grouse

Peregrines, whether tiercel or falcon, are the perfect match for grouse, although there is some risk of very small tiercels seriously damaging their feet in repeatedly hitting such a tough quarry. All too often, pink marks on a tiercel's feet show the bruising caused by cutting over an old cock grouse. Although the number of grouse in the bag at the end of the day should not be the only criteria by which to judge the excellence of a grouse hawk, records clearly show that eyasses, and in particular well hacked eyasses, have, over the years, proved the more reliable,

Peregrine tiercel on grouse

consistent and successful as game hawks. As a general rule there is no doubt that both tiercels and small falcons will learn to wait-on more easily than large, heavy falcons, and they will also usually go very much higher. They obviously realise that they need height to compensate for being slower than large falcons in level flight. Many large falcons do not mount so high, relying on their greater speed to catch their quarry. Grouse seem to be more frightened of the larger hawks and are more likely to drop to the ground to evade a stoop in front of a big falcon or gyr than when they are being pursued by a tiercel.

Grouse hawking with gyrs

Most early falconers wrote off the gyr as a possible game hawk. It was said that they were too impatient to wait-on, were difficult to hood and even more difficult to keep in good health and flying condition. During the last decade a few gyrs have disproved these ideas, and the exploits at grouse of such hawks as 'Dovre', a captive-bred eyas jerkin, have shown the potential of these handsome hawks. While it has to be said that this jerkin certainly took his time to learn to wait-on, he became one of the most consistent and high waiting-on grouse hawks to be flown on the grouse moors of Scotland in recent years. Although he was unhacked he would fly as strongly on the first day of each season as he had finished the previous year, which would seem to disprove the theory that large hawks, and in particular gyrs, require a long time to get fit at the start of each season.

However, there are some large peregrines and other gyrs that seem to need several weeks of work before they are at their best. Jerkins are certainly worthy of being included in the list of suitable hawks to fly at grouse, but once they are proficient at the game they might be more than a match for grouse because of their great strength and speed. As with peregrines, a hacked jerkin would probably be more successful at quarry than an unhacked brother. Gyrs are inclined to sit about far more than peregrines when at hack. To overcome this it is worth experimenting by putting one jerkin out to hack with a group of peregrines to see if he follows their example and takes more exercise. The female gyr can take grouse in the easiest possible style, perhaps too easily to be sporting. However, if black game could be found in sufficient numbers, their greater size and speed would better balance the mighty gyrfalcon.

Flying other types of hawk at grouse

Sakers have been flown successfully at grouse, but they do not like the strong winds so often met with on the moors. Sakers mount well and will wait-on, but those very few that have been tried have been found wanting in the ability to punch forward against a strong head-wind. They are good footers and are clever and quick on the ground. Shahins and Barbary falcons have been tried and are quite capable of catching grouse, although they are perhaps rather more easily discouraged. One or two lanners have caught grouse, but they would probably be better suited for flying at the smaller and slower partridge.

Black game and ptarmigan as quarry

Black game are found on some grouse moors; indeed the greyhen and her young do not at first seem noticeably different from a covey of grouse when they rise in front of a point. Young and female black game are rather more easily taken by a hawk than grouse because they rarely shift from the stoop with the same agility and, although fast, they are easily bound-to. Adult black cock can also be taken in the stoop by a hawk which is bold and strong enough to tackle such a large bird, weighing as much as double that of the biggest grouse. However, although they appear not to shift from the stoop in the same way as their red brethren, they are certainly faster once they are well on the wing (they seem to change from the rhythm of a game-like flight to a slower wing-beat, almost goose-like, once they are well up in the air), and can pull away from the fastest of peregrines in a stern chase.

Ptarmigan are rather smaller than the red grouse and are usually found in very rugged country (over 2,000 feet), which is far from ideal country in which to fly a favourite falcon. Nevertheless, the excitement of catching a ptarmigan has tempted three or four intrepid falconers to the high tops in recent years, and their enthusiasm has been well rewarded.

Partridge hawking

Partridge are flown in much the same way as grouse, except that the dog need not play such a major part in the day's sport. Partridge can be found without the use of a 'bird' dog, either by walking them up or by driving through the stubble in a car. Although the partridge covey might flush on seeing the hawking party, they do not fly as far or as fast as grouse, and they can usually be marked down again at no great distance. With a car, the covey can often be spotted running ahead of the vehicle. Drive a little way away from them before stopping the car. Then get one of the party to keep an eye on where you know the partridge are, because if you take your eye off them they might well slip away unseen and there will be nothing there when you fly your hawk.

Once the partridge are marked down, the hawk should be flown. When the hawk has reached her pitch, the falconer and his friends should walk in line down wind to flush the quarry. However, partridge can hide on the barest of ground and the falconer should at least use a spaniel to try and ensure that he doesn't walk over them. Since partridge are not as fast as grouse, it is not quite so important to flush them down wind. Even though a down wind stoop will have more power behind it, the hawk should run up to the partridge with little difficulty provided that she is high enough. Partridge hawks need not wait-on as high as grouse hawks; indeed, if the enclosures are small it is better to flush the partridge before the hawk has reached her proper pitch so that she may

Fig. 134 (above) A tiercel binding-to partridge which are 'skying up' from a flush

Fig. 135 (right) Tiercel stooping directly at partridge that are flying well above the ground

get in her stoop before the game gets to cover. Particularly later on in the season, partridge 'sky up' when flushed, thus giving the hawk an opportunity either to easily scoop them up from behind or to stoop straight into the covey to cut over a chosen bird. Also, a covey of partridge will tend to scatter from the stoop, making it possible for various individual birds to be marked down for further flights.

Driving partridge on to hawking ground

Gilbert Blaine used to drive partridge off the open downland with a line of beaters so that they put in to root fields which afforded rather more cover. Once the beaters had come up, a hawk would be flown and allowed to reach his pitch over the crops. Next, the beaters would begin slowly driving out the turnips with an old setter and a spaniel or two working ahead of them.

However, a hawk that has been flown at grouse in the early part of the season and has learned to wait-on over a pointing dog, is better served if a pointer or setter is used to find the partridge.

Hawking over a dog

Game hawking, whether at partridge or pheasant, is more enjoyable when using a pointing dog to find the game. With grouse it is essential. Hawks learn to understand the dog so well that some will only wait-on over a dog that is actually pointing. They soon see that a dog which is beating back and across the hill is unlikely to flush a grouse, and that it is only when the dog stops and points that the appearance of grouse is imminent.

An old haggard falcon, 'Jallad', who flew at grouse with distinction for more than twelve seasons, became very cunning towards the end, such that if the dog was running she would sit up on a convenient rock or fence post. As soon as the dog came on point the falcon would beat low across the heather until she was upwind of the dog. There she would mount to her pitch from which she would usually neatly cut over a grouse.

In practice there is some risk involved in grouse hawking in that the hawk will usually only need to wait-on over the dog for a very short period before the grouse are flushed. Once a hawk has become reliable at waiting-on, it is sensible, on occasion, to keep her waiting some time before flushing to show her that waiting is worth while. After mounting well over the pointing dog, some hawks will quickly lose interest in the proceedings if the dog takes a great deal of time in locating the grouse in front of the point. Ironically, a hawk will probably learn to be more patient if she is flown over a dog that invariably takes its time in accurately locating and flushing grouse rather than a dog that is clever and fast at finding the quarry.

Both tiercels and falcons (peregrines) can be successfully flown at partridge, although the tiercel has long been regarded as the neater opponent. The falcon is more than a match for the partridge and can easily carry such small quarry. If a falcon binds-to her partridge she may well carry it for some distance before settling, and a great deal of time can be wasted searching for her. Even worse, the falcon may repeatedly lift her quarry each time the falconer approaches her, with much of the day being spent recovering her. Once a hawk has lifted and carried her partridge she is even more likely to do so when approached a second time. A hawk will find it easier to carry her quarry on a windy day, particularly if she lands on a hillside. (For recovering a hawk see the section on snipe hawking, page 160).

Suitable country

Partridge can be flown in any type of country which is open enough to give a waiting-on hawk sufficient room to come up to the quarry in the stoop before they reach cover. Nevertheless, however large the enclosures are, all too often game are found near to a hedge, a fence or a copse. It is often possible to flush partridge so that, hopefully, they put down in a more suitable area for a flight. Grey partridge do not drop in front of a hawk in the same way as grouse, and they do not run on putting in unless they are in thick cover.

Flying at red-legged partridge

If it can be persuaded to fly at the right moment, the red-legged partridge is also a rewarding quarry. Like the grey partridge, it will 'sky up' in front of a hawk, thus allowing a good hawk to cut over one partridge while binding-to another from the same covey. Red-legged partridge will run ahead of the dogs in the barest of cover, and many European falconers have found it necessary to fly their hawks before running their dogs in an effort to 'hold' the partridge so that both the dogs and the falconers can get up to flush them. Hawks which are accustomed to being flown in this way will often wait-on at a great height for half-an-hour or more, having learned that they will only be served with quarry if they wait.

Pheasant hawking

When partridge hawking over dogs you can never be certain whether it is a partridge or a pheasant in front of the dog. Although the pheasant is

Fig. 136 A hawk stooping behind and up to a rising pheasant

fast it doesn't shift from the stoop in the same way as grouse or partridge, but climbs away like an aircraft when heading for cover. Provided that a hawk is brave enough to tackle such large quarry, pheasants are easily caught, but they are not such a rewarding quarry as either grouse or partridge for long winged hawks. Of course, there is quite a difference between wild-bred pheasants out in open country, and reared birds flushed out of sugar beet, kale or low game cover early in October or November. Some hawks will regularly take the smaller hen pheasant but will resolutely refuse to take a tough old cock. Although many tiercels take them well, some of the smaller hawks, tiercels, Barbarys or lannerets might well decline to fly at pheasants; they are a rough, tough customer on the ground and cocks will face up to an uncertain hawk like a fighting game-cock, fully prepared to do battle. Once they have been flushed from cover, pheasants invariably climb away, gaining height, and thus they are readily taken by a hawk that stoops behind them, sweeps up and follows the line of flight to bind to them with contemptuous ease.

Snipe hawking

Both snipe and woodcock can provide some variety when out grouse hawking. They may also be found on some partridge ground. Snipe are easily taken early in the season by a hawk that is waiting-on, and if bound-to they do not hinder the hawk's flight at all. 'Old Bitch' once neatly bound-to a snipe and proceeded to eat it while waiting-on, not bothering to put down to eat such a tiny morsel.

Although a well-trained hawk should not wish to carry her quarry away from the approaching falconer, even the best mannered of hawks might be tempted to carry a snipe. However, should your hawk eat the snipe before you manage to take her up she will still have sufficient appetite to come to the lure or a dead grouse. If your hawk does carry a snipe, it is better to let her eat it rather than encourage further carrying by approaching her. If she allows you within some yards of her, then throw the lure or a dead grouse at her and she may well transfer her attention to the larger meal. With a long lure line or a creance tied to the dead grouse or lure, you can manoeuvre it so that it is right against the feet of the hawk, even covering the snipe. Then you can take your hawk up in the normal way.

Later in the season snipe will often evade the first stoop of a hawk to rocket away into the sky closely followed by the hawk. The snipe well might keep on climbing until the hawk gives up the pursuit, but if hard pressed it will eventually drop like a stone for cover, and might well be snatched up just as it attempts to do so.

Woodcock hawking

Although they are not usually found in heather, woodcock often take cover in bracken in hollows on the moor. While they are not particularly difficult to take in the first stoop, woodcock will, on dodging the first attack, take to the sky, resulting in an enjoyable, high, zig-zagging or ringing flight that will test the qualities of the very best of hawks. Unfortunately, one can never be sure whether the dog is pointing a grouse, a pheasant or a woodcock in bracken. Thus it may be better to flush the quarry and mark them down as well as possible in cover. A hawk can then be flown and a dog put in to flush the quarry.

Woodcock will run through bracken and may well be found eventually, if at all, a very long way from where they put in. The hawk must wait patiently and keep a close position overhead to succeed at this quarry. Some pointers will not acknowledge woodcock, and will neither point them nor indeed retrieve them. The very few woodcock that my hawks have managed to take have all resulted from a hunted grouse putting into bracken, with the woodcock flushing by chance as the dogs hunted out the grouse.

Duck hawking

Duck can be hawked from small lochs, ponds or splashes with a hawk that waits-on. Teal are often to be found on tiny lochans on the boggy grouse moors of Caithness, and they afford an excellent flight. Most species of duck can be hawked provided that they can be found far enough from any large or deep stretch of water into which they could crash in full flight, leaving the hawk covered in spray. Even if you found the duck again they would be almost impossible to re-flush from such water. Streams, dykes or burns are just as difficult because the duck will repeatedly drop into the water just ahead of the hawk. If the stretch of water is small enough, the duck can be hunted out, but it will then drop in again further and further down the water until either the hawk, the duck or the falconer runs out of steam. Mallard are strong and fast and provide excellent sport for the larger hawks. Tiercel peregrines can take mallard but, after taking one, many never take another, having received a severe buffeting on the ground.

7

Glove and hood making

Most of the equipment needed by the falconer is simple in design and, provided that he has some skill with scissors, needles and knife, he should be able to make at least some of it at home. However, a certain number of tools is needed, and leather, normally only available in half or whole skins, demands a considerable financial investment which in most cases would be better spent buying the furniture that is required.

Fortunately, there are now a number of professional or part-time suppliers of falconry furniture. Many of these suppliers carry a comprehensive range of things that might possibly be needed by the falconer, and they also produce well-crafted and workmanlike equipment at practical prices. When ordering furniture it is as well to remember that proven designs and patterns are better for use in the field and that, while 'only the best is good enough' for the dedicated falconer, the best is not necessarily the most ornate or expensive.

For those who wish to make up some of their own falconry furniture, particularly gloves, jesses, hoods and other leather work, the following tools and materials are recommended:

leather scissors: 6in (15cm)
Stanley knife
saddler's awl with assorted blades
revolving punch pliers
pricking iron: ½in (13mm);
    8 stitch marks to the inch
chisels: ³⁄₁₆in (4.75mm)/¼in
    (6mm)/½in (13mm)

gloving needles no. 1 or 2
saddler's needles no. 2 to 5
beeswax
linen thread, reverse twist
no. 18/3 cord
no. 25/3 cord
Copydex glue
veterinary tweezers or artery
    forceps

(see the section on Aylmeri jesses for eyelets and tools)

Gloves

Hawking gloves are not difficult to make, provided that the instructions are carefully followed and that suitable leather, tools and patterns are available. Nevertheless, some skill at stitching is needed and it is probably easier and almost as cheap to buy a custom-made glove. The ideal leather is deerskin, doeskin, reindeer skin or dingo skin, that is leather which is supple and yet strong. However, the best quality deerskin is very expensive, and care should be taken in cutting so that the

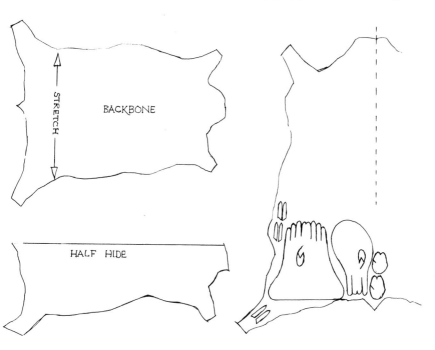

Fig. 137 Skin showing 'stretch', that is the strongest leather along the backbone

Fig. 138 The pattern for a double-layer glove correctly placed on the skin with the 'stretch' across the glove

maximum number of gloves may be obtained. The strongest and thickest leather in an unsplit skin is along the line of the backbone of the animal, while the thinnest and softest leather is at the sides of the hide.

The pattern should be placed on the skin so that the natural stretch of the leather is across the glove. It is easy to mark around the patterns with a biro. Make sure that the pattern is the right way up so that you cut out your glove and finish with the preferred surface on the outside. Most falconers prefer to have the flesh or sueded side of the skin on the outside of their glove. It is surprisingly easy to end up with a right-handed glove when you really needed a left-handed one. It is also easy to cut out the thumb piece the wrong way round, so remember to mark your patterns.

For the larger hawks it is normal practice to double the leather over the thumb, the first one or two fingers and part of the cuff. Cut out the glove pieces with a sharp pair of leather scissors (do not cut any other material, particularly paper or card, with your leather scissors since this will blunt them), but before cutting out the thumb, stick two layers of leather together so that the edges will be neat and will match. Glue the second layer of leather over the two fingers and the cuff of the glove; this will make it very much easier to stitch the layer to the glove. Now cut the thumb-hole out as marked on the pattern.

RUNNING STITCH

GLOVING or STAB STITCH

Fig. 139 The correct gloving stitch and an incorrect running stitch

Fig. 140 The gloving knot

Wax a length of no. 18/3 cord linen thread with your block of beeswax and stitch around the edge of the second layer of leather to secure it to the main part of the glove. Use a no. 1 or 2 gloving needle. The correct stitch is a stab or gloving stitch – not a running stitch. Keep your stitches small, neat and in line. With practice you will find that your stitches are nearly all of a similar size and spacing, but while you are a beginner a faint pencil line might help you to keep your stitches the same distance from the edge of the leather. To finish off a run of stitching tie a gloving knot, that is a half-hitch, around the thread so that the knot is tight up against the glove.

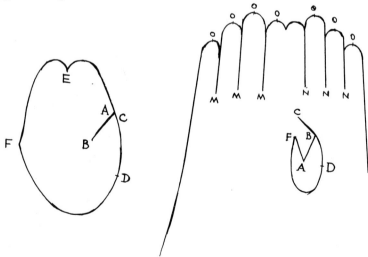

Fig. 141 A pattern showing the order of figures in stitching the thumb section on to the glove

Next, sew in the thumb piece. Place the edges A–B to A–B. Start stitching from A and using neat, tight stitches work towards point B. Twist the thumb piece around so that B–C can be held against B–C, then continue stitching to C. Once again twist the thumb piece and stitch to point D. Knot off the thread on the inside of the glove.

Start stitching again at point E (you will now begin to see how the thumb piece finally fits into place) and stitch to point F. Continue on around the curve of the thumb, easing the leather if necessary to fit neatly together, until you meet up with your previous stitching at point D. Overlap one stitch and knot off inside as before. If you find it easier you can touch the edges together with glue as you proceed. The thumb is the most difficult part in stitching up a glove and if you can master that the rest will be easy. Keep the stitches small, neat and tight so that there is less chance of a hawk getting a claw through a seam.

Alternatively, you could sew the two thumb pieces to each separate layer of leather before gluing them together, as it were pulling one glove on top of the other. However, this creates a clumsy and bulky finish to the glove. The patterns must be very accurately cut so that the one will fit over the other, and because the outer seam should be directly over the inner seam there is still a chance that a hawk claw might prick you through the seam.

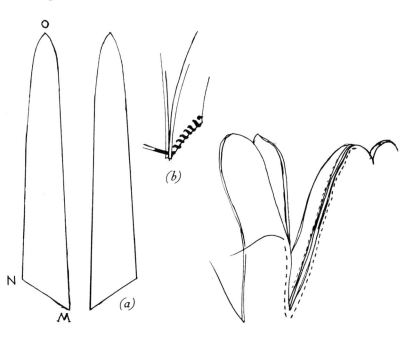

Fig. 142 A pair of fourchettes shown separately (a) and oversewn together (b)

Fig. 143 A pair of fourchettes that have been sewn between the first and second fingers on the back of a glove

Glove and hood making

The six fourchettes, that is the shaped pieces that fit between the fingers, are also cut from the leather with the stretch across their width. The fourchettes are stitched to the fingers up the back of the hand, with the first pair that fits between the first and second fingers being slightly wider and of stronger leather than the others. Each pair is over-sewn across the base from points N–M, and the thread is taken through point M on the back of the glove at the base of first and second fingers. The fourchette is then stitched up the side of the first finger towards point O. Knot off after making sure that you have finished stitching just short of the centre top of the finger and have shaped the top of the fourchette to fit neatly in place. Return to point M and stitch towards point O on the second finger. Repeat the exercise with the other two pairs of fourchettes between the second and the third fingers and between the third and the little finger.

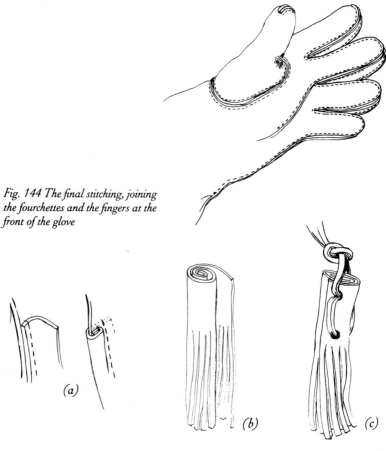

Fig. 144 The final stitching, joining the fourchettes and the fingers at the front of the glove

(a)

(b)

(c)

Fig. 145 (a) Binding the raw edge of the cuff with leather. (b) A tassle which has been cut and rolled. (c) A tassle ready for knotting to the glove

Next, fold the glove and stitch the front of the fingers to the fourchettes with a long, waxed thread, starting at the top of the first finger and working round each finger in turn. Ensure that the joined bottom of the fourchettes at point N fits neatly at point N on the glove. Finally, from the top of the little finger sew the front and the back of the glove together down the side, and knot off where you want the cuff opening to start. The raw edge of the leather around the cuff can be bound with a contrasting leather and trimmed with a loop of leather or a tassle.

Jesses

Traditional jesses can be cut from a variety of leathers. Kangaroo skin is excellent, provided that it is kept well greased. Calfskin does nearly as well and dingo skin or buckskin are also ideal. Buckskin or deerskin (as used for glove making) does not go hard when wet as easily as most leathers, but it also benefits from regular greasing. Kho-cho-line is excellent as a dressing for jesses and leashes, or you could make up a special mix at home, using one measure of beeswax to two measures of candles together with liquid paraffin. To prepare this mix, slowly melt the beeswax and the candlewax over a low heat, then add the liquid paraffin and stir it in. Let it cool, but melt it again and add more paraffin if it is too stiff to spread easily over the leather.

Cut strips of leather for jesses or leashes parallel to the backbone of the skin and wider than necessary. Next, grease the strips and stretch them before cutting them to the required length and shape. Punch holes at the end of each slit in the jess with the smallest punch on the revolving punch pliers. Use a sharp chisel to cut the slits and carefully note the exact arrangement of slits as shown in Chapter 2 and in the patterns.

Aylmeri jesses

The leather should be treated and cut as with traditional jesses, but be careful not to cut too large a hole for the eyelets; they should be a tight fit. (The following measurements are given according to manufacturer's specifications.) For goshawk-sized Aylmeri (E) use brass sail eyelets with turnover rings (no. 25B: $^{7}/_{16}$in closed diameter). To cut the hole use a no. 13 round punch and a sail eyelet closing tool no. 25. For a peregrine/saker (F) use eyelet no. 23B: $^{11}/_{32}$in and a no. 11 round punch. For a peregrine tiercel (G) use eyelet no. 22B: $^{5}/_{16}$in and a no. 10 round punch. For a sparrowhawk/merlin (H) use a $^{5}/_{32}$in Rimmon eyelet and a no. 6 round punch or a $^{9}/_{32}$in Mogul eyelet and no. 7 round punch. (The Rimmon and Mogul eyelets are closed with eyelet pliers.)

The best rivets to use for type F Aylmeri jesses are brass, tubular rivets (stems and caps) with a 7mm stem and a cap of 6 or 7mm. For extra large jesses use a 9 or 10mm stem, and a 7mm cap. These rivets can be either crushed together with pliers or tapped with a hammer against a metal block.

Hoods

Arab hoods

Arab hoods can be be made up in calf or goatskin. If it is not too heavy shoe hide is also suitable. Sew up the hood inside out, then turn it back the right way and either flatten the seam with a hammer over a mould, or dampen it and rub it on the work-top with your thumb or finger inside the hood. If you find it easier you can glue each seam ahead of the stitching. With thinner leathers it is best to hold the leather face-to-face, and either over-sew or use a stab or prix stitch. With more substantial leather you can stitch edge-to-edge so that the stitching is hidden in the thickness of the leather. The final size of the hood may be altered easily by varying the distance the stitching is from the edge of the leather and by changing the type of stitch that is used.

Fig. 146 (a) Stab or prix stitch. (b) Oversewing   *Fig. 147 Stitching leather edge-to-edge with a split stitch*

Dutch hood

The Dutch hood or Syrio-Dutch hood is cut out in three separate pieces from a modelling hide or calfskin. Before attempting to make up this type of hood you need to carve or mould a set of wooden or fibre glass hood blocks over which the hood is then moulded.

Fig. 148 Hood blocks

These hoods are by far the most difficult for the beginner to make up at home, and on the whole they are better left to the professional hood-makers. The side panels are covered in a baize cloth or sueded leather, which is glued on, allowing enough overlap to be drawn into the seam when sewing up the hood. This effectively prevents light showing through the seams. It is easier to stitch the hoods inside out, with the stitch remaining hidden in the thickness of the leather.

The Dutch hood-makers always used over-sew stitches, but today hood-makers use very neat stab or saddle stitching. Before knotting off the thread, wet the hood, turn it right side out and tighten up the stitches. Wet the hood again and mould it over the hood block. The Dutch hood proper is bound around the neck-opening with a strip of fine skiver leather.

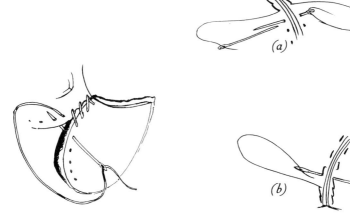

Fig. 149 Over-stitching the side panel to the body of a Dutch hood

Fig. 150 (a) Saddle stitching with two needles. (b) Back stitching with a single needle

Anglo–Indian hoods

Anglo-Indian hoods are the easiest of the different styles of hood to make at home. The leather should be fairly thin but stiff. Good quality aniline calf and goatskin, such as are used for bookbinding, or pigskin are all suitable. The hood is normally sewn on the outside and it is better to use a saddle stitch or backstitch, marking and making the holes before stitching with your saddler's awl. If the awl is held at an angle when making the holes the leather will bulge out more easily over the eye when stitched. It can also be slightly moulded with the thumb or forefinger after stitching.

Fig. 151 A Turkistan eagle hood showing how the throat lash is fitted

Eagle hoods

The Turkistan eagle hood pattern is made up in the same way as an Anglo-Indian hood, but as can be seen from the pattern, the throat piece is cut separately. After the hood is sewn up the throat piece is threaded through the slits provided, doubled over, then glued and sewn.

Braces

Braces should be cut rather wider than the brace slits in the back of the hood and also longer than necessary, because some length is lost in making the button. The braces are not sewn to the hood but are threaded in a cunning way through three slits cut either side of the hood. The long or closing end of each brace is then threaded through the two outer slits where the opposite brace is attached to the hood.

Fig. 152 Braces

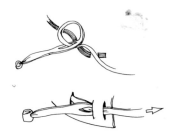

Fig. 153 A brace threaded through three slits at the back of the hood

Fig. 154 The long end of the brace is threaded through two slits from the opposite side

Trimming

Arab and Anglo-Indian hoods are traditionally trimmed with a tag or plume of leather which makes a convenient handle when hooding a hawk. The Dutch hood normally has a rather more fancy plume made up with feathers and wool, and bound with brass wire.

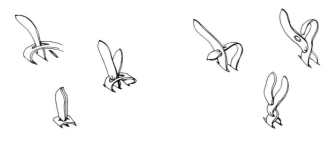

Fig. 155 A simple tag is threaded through three slits in the top of the hood to form a plume/handle

Fig. 156 A leather tag acting as a plume/handle on a hood

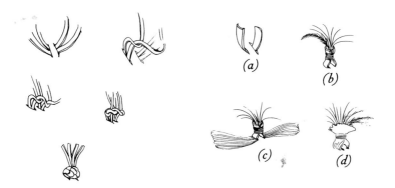

Fig. 157 How to make a Turk's head knot

Fig. 158 (a) A leather tag is threaded through slits in the hood. (b) Feathers are bound to the tag. (c) Wool is threaded through the slits. (d) The wool is bound with brass wire

Lures

Lures are best made up in leather or rubber (see Chapter 2 and the patterns). They come in as many varieties as do hoods, but whatever shape and size you choose, make sure that the swivel is securely anchored to the lure. You can do this by sewing a heavy Terylene webbing well down into the body of the lure. A light lure can be padded with upholstery foam or saddle flocking. For a heavier lure a piece of lead which is well wrapped and padded will soon add weight.

The strings on the lure should be made of strong nylon cord (renewed every season), and these are best knotted right through the body of the lure, using a round punch or a large sacking needle. If the lure is to be garnished with dried or cured birds' wings it is advisable to add an additional 'plate' of leather to the lure on which meat can be tied.

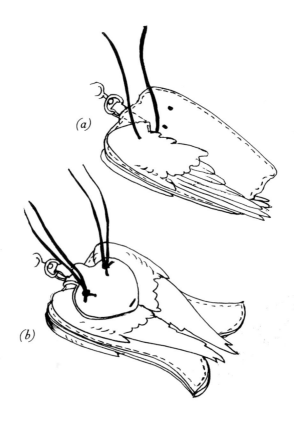

Fig. 159 Lures. (a) A dried wing is tied into position on this lure. (b) This lure has a 'plate' of leather on to which meat may be tied

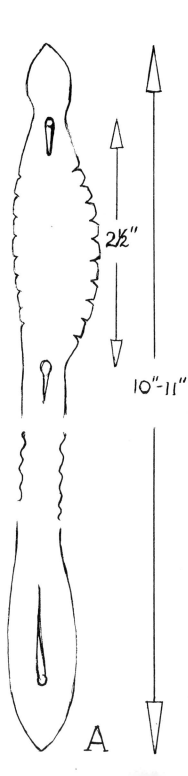

8
Patterns

2½"

10"-11"

A

1 Jesses. (a) Suitable for goshawks, Red-tail buzzards etc. (b) *(page 174)* Suitable for a peregrine falcon, saker etc. (c) Suitable for a peregrine tiercel. (d) Suitable for a merlin

2 Aylmeri jesses. (e) *(page 175)* Suitable for a goshawk. (f) Suitable for a peregrine falcon. (g) *(page 176)* Suitable for a peregrine tiercel. (h) Suitable for a sparrowhawk

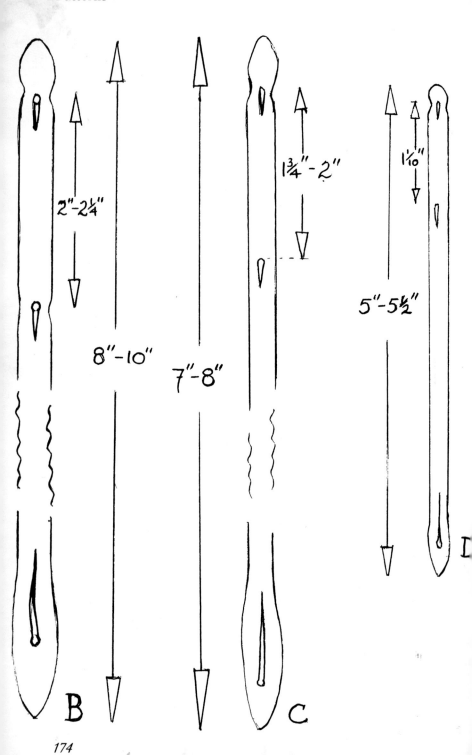

2"–2¼"

8"–10"

7"–8"

1¾"–2"

1⅒"

5"–5½"

B

C

D

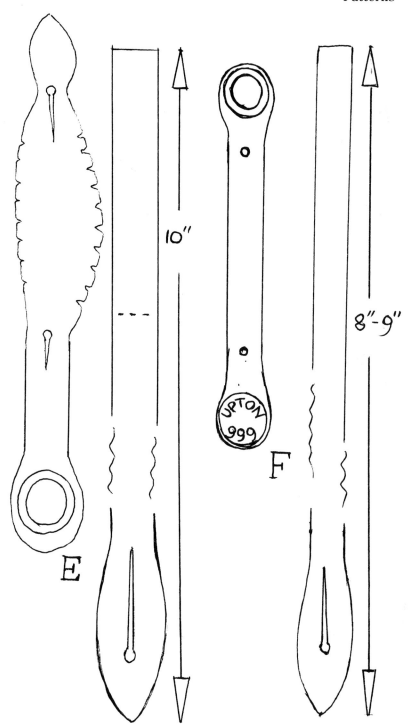

E

10"

F

8"-9"

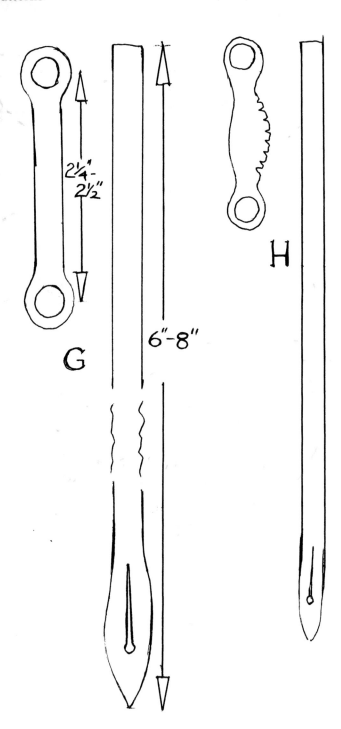

$2\frac{1}{4}"-$
$2\frac{1}{2}"$

G

$6"-8"$

H

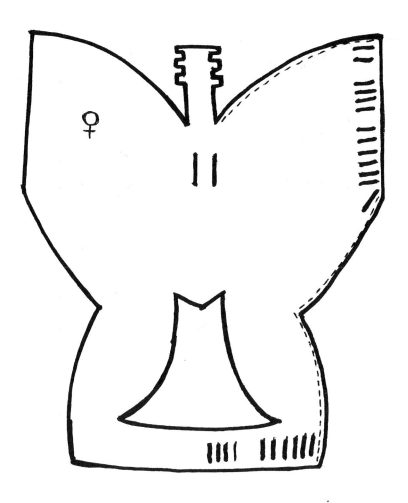

Indian hood pattern from the Panjab, suitable for a peregrine falcon

Patterns

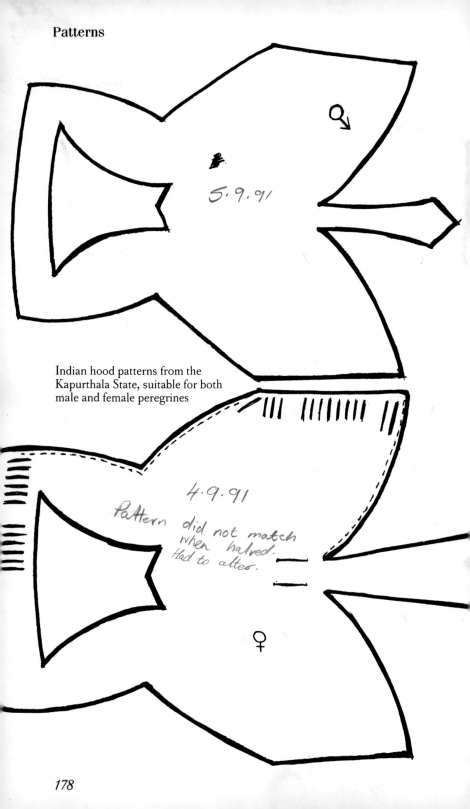

5.9.91

Indian hood patterns from the
Kapurthala State, suitable for both
male and female peregrines

4.9.91

Pattern did not match
when halved.
Had to alter.

178

Indian hood patterns

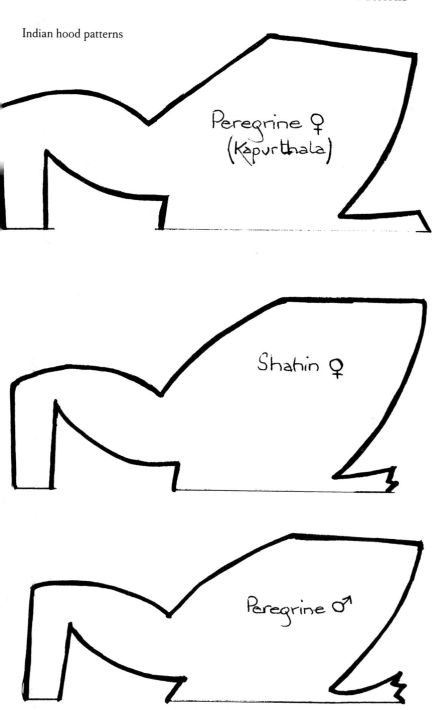

Peregrine ♀
(Kapurthala)

Shahin ♀

Peregrine ♂

Patterns

Saker

Peregrine

Lagar ♀

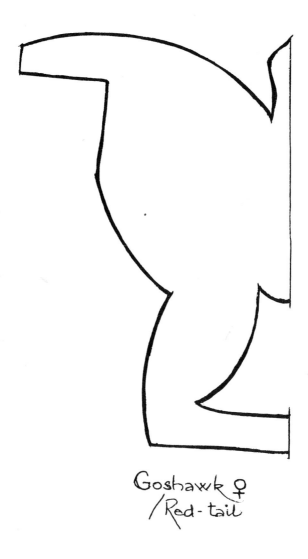

Goshawk ♀
/ Red-tail

Left and above Anglo-Indian hood patterns

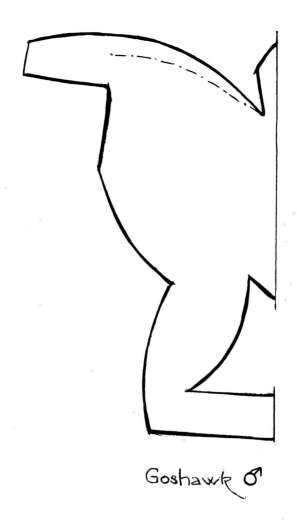

Goshawk ♂

Anglo-Indian pattern

1. Stu's Keo 6.9.91.

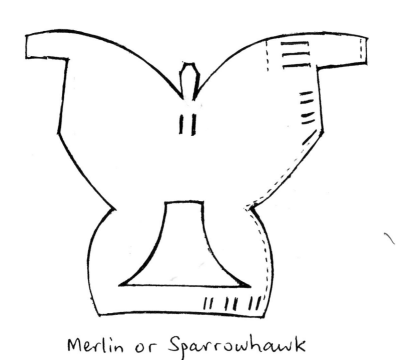

Merlin or Sparrowhawk

Anglo-Indian pattern

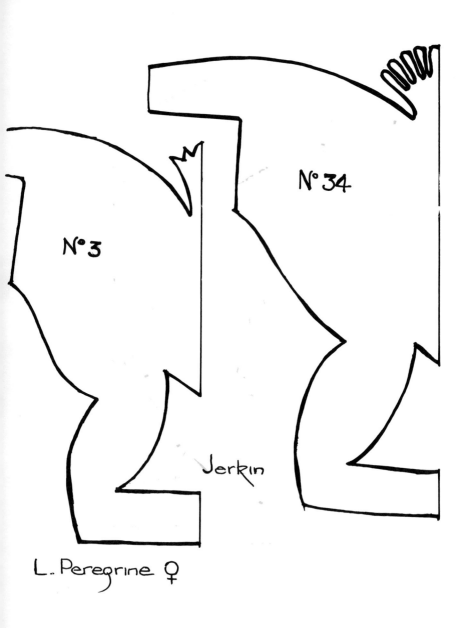

N° 3

N° 34

Jerkin

L. Peregrine ♀

Anglo Indian patterns (*Note* The
numbers on the following patterns
represent the author's pattern sizes.)

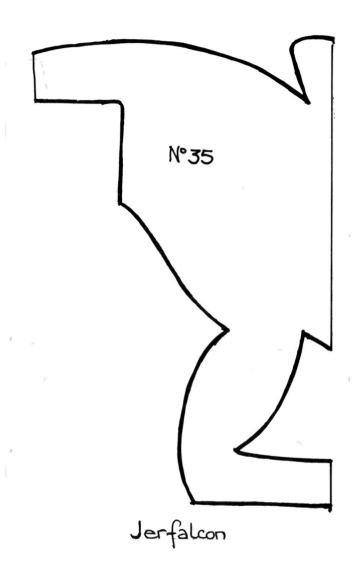

N° 35

Jerfalcon

Anglo-Indian pattern

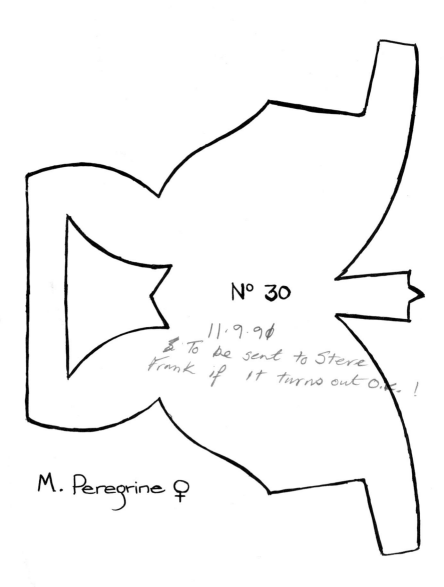

Nº 30

11·9·9∅

⅜ To be sent to Steve
Frank if it turns out O.K.!

M. Peregrine ♀

Above and right Anglo-Indian patterns

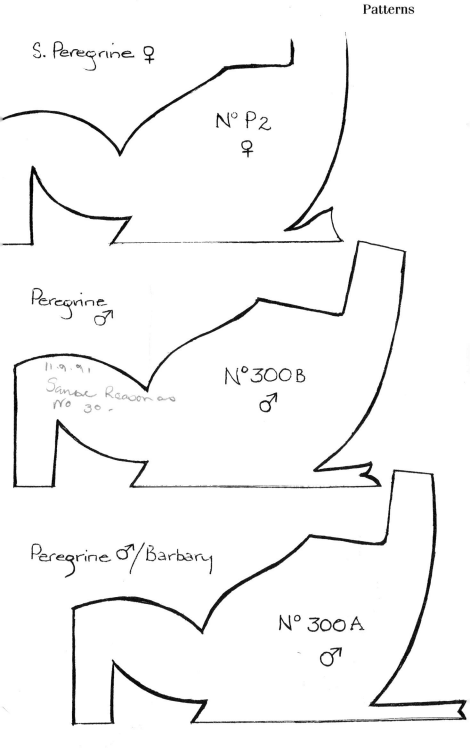

S. Peregrine ♀

N° P2
♀

Peregrine
♂

11.9.91
Same Reason as
No 30.

N° 300 B
♂

Peregrine ♂/Barbary

N° 300 A
♂

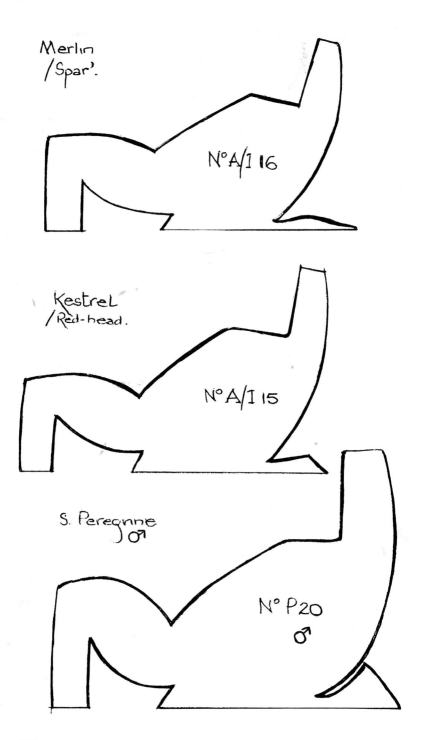

Merlin /Spar'.

N°A/I 16

Kestrel /Red-head.

N°A/I 15

S. Peregrine ♂

N° P20 ♂

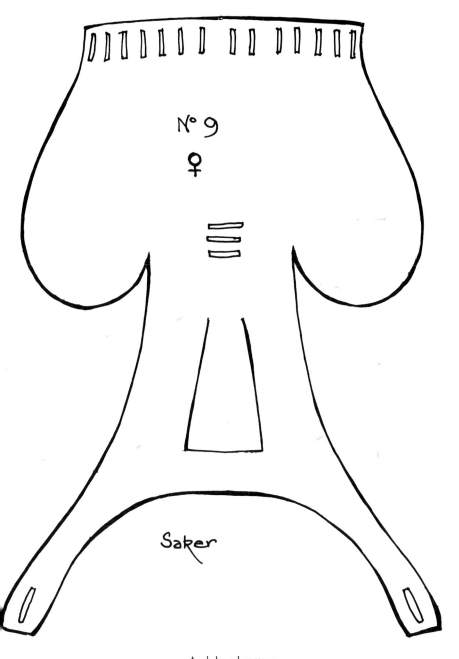

N° 9

♀

Saker

Arab hood pattern

Left Anglo-Indian patterns

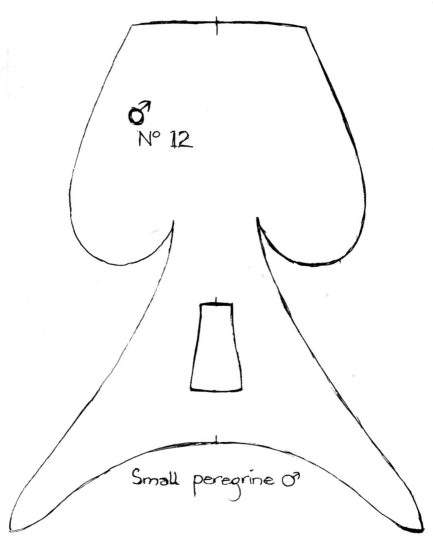

♂

N° 12

Small peregrine ♂

Above and right Arab patterns

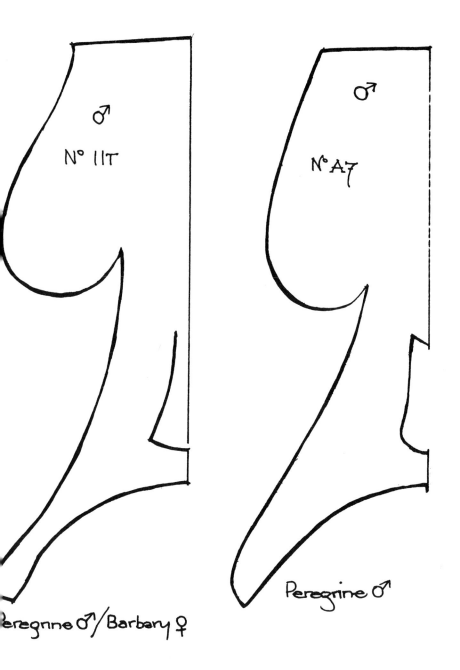

♂

N° IIT

Peregrine ♂ / Barbary ♀

♂

N° A7

Peregrine ♂

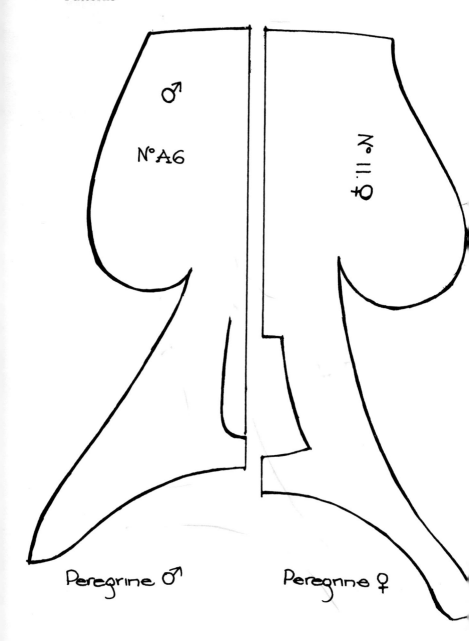

♂

N° A6

N° 11 ♂

Peregrine ♂   Peregrine ♀

Arab pattern

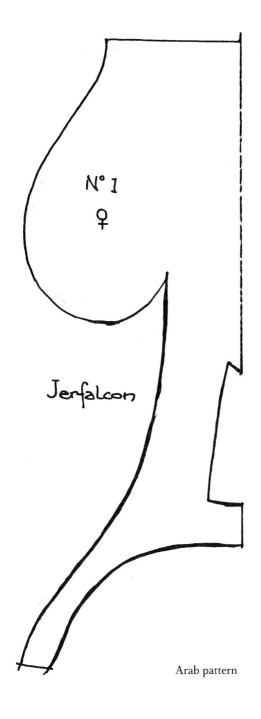

N° 1

♀

Jerfalcon

Arab pattern

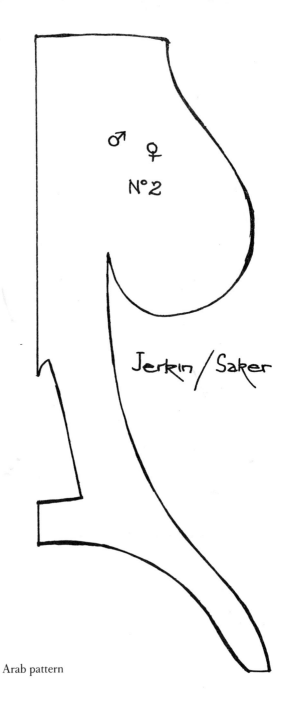

♂   ♀

N° 2

Jerkin / Saker

Arab pattern

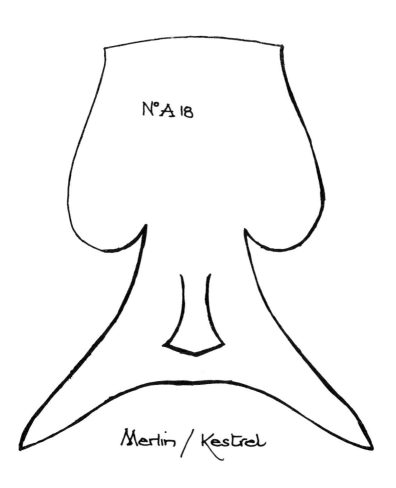

N° A 18

Merlin / Kestrel

Arab pattern

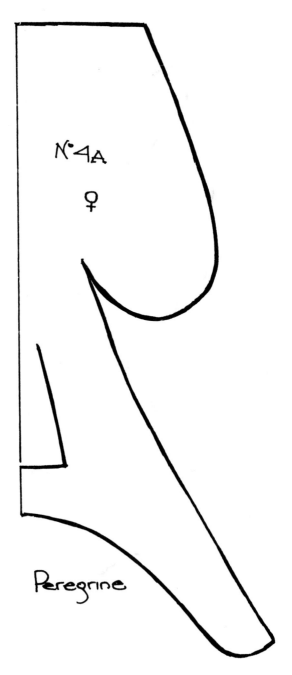

N°4A

♀

Peregrine

Arab pattern

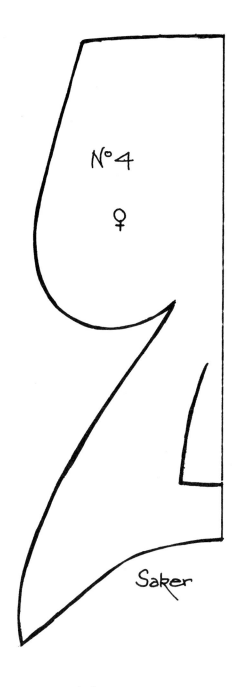

N°4

♀

Saker

Arab pattern

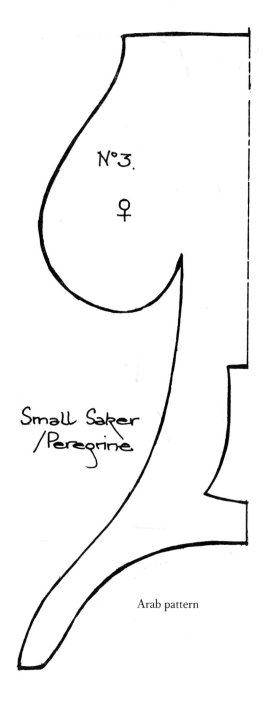

N°3.

♀

Small Saker
/Peregrine

Arab pattern

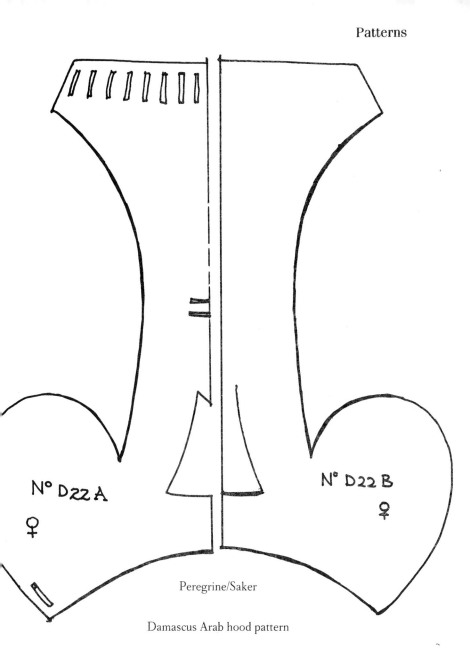

N° D22 A

♀

N° D22 B

♀

Peregrine/Saker

Damascus Arab hood pattern

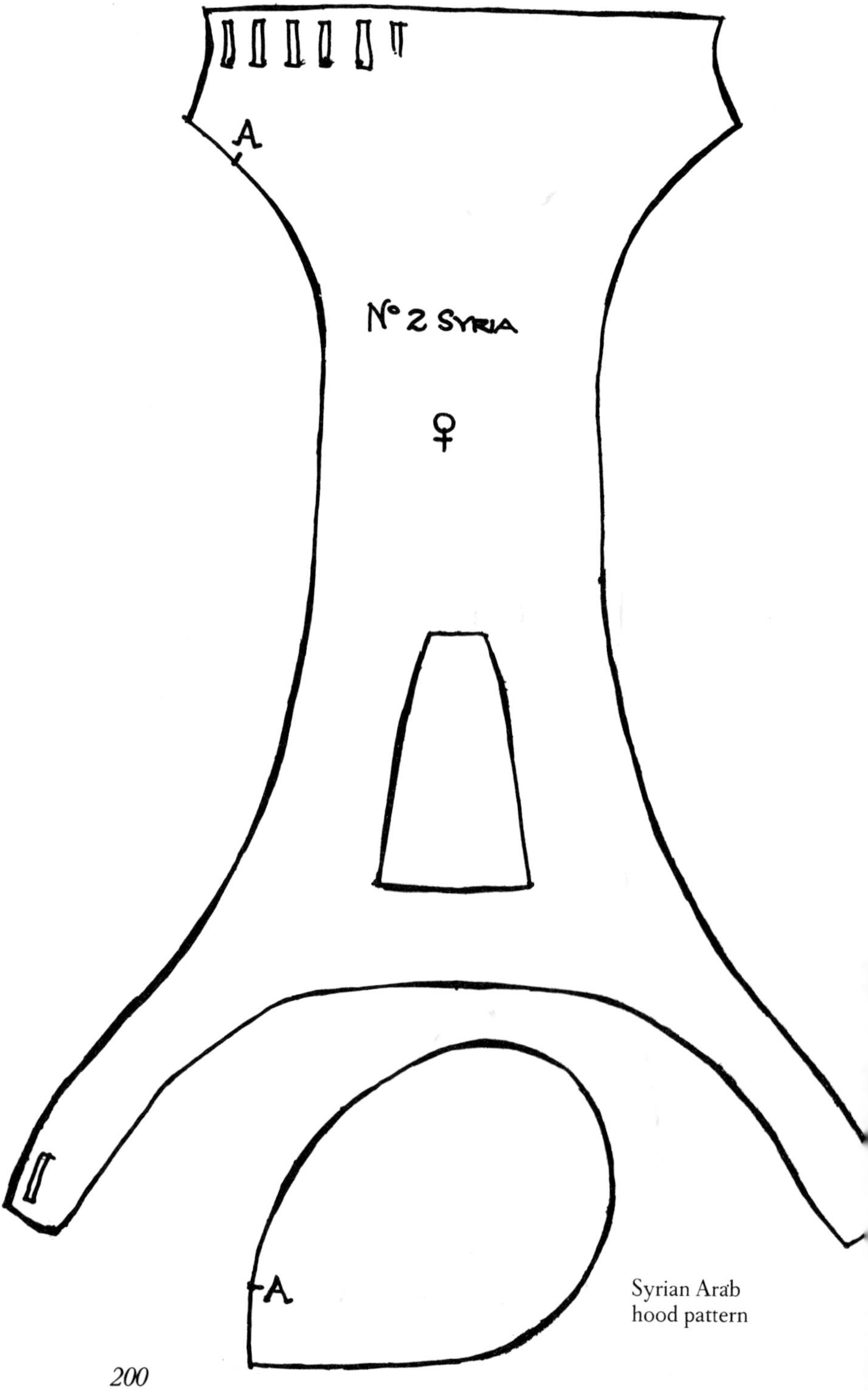

N° 2 SYRIA

♀

Syrian Arab
hood pattern

A

A

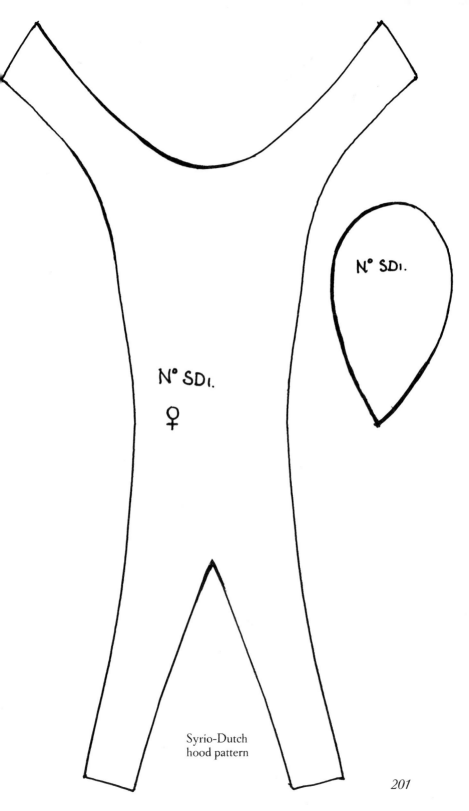

N° SD1.

N° SD1.
♀

Syrio-Dutch
hood pattern

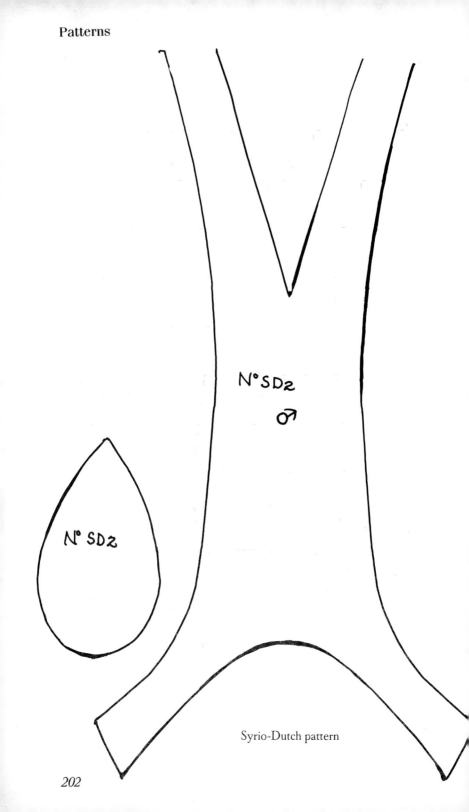

N° SD2
♂

N° SD2

Syrio-Dutch pattern

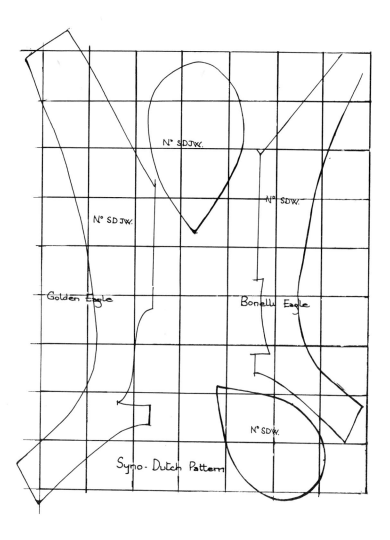

Nº SDJW.

Nº SD JW.

Nº SDW.

Golden Eagle

Bonelli Eagle

Nº SDW.

Syno-Dutch Pattern

Enlarge to 1″ (2.5cm) squares

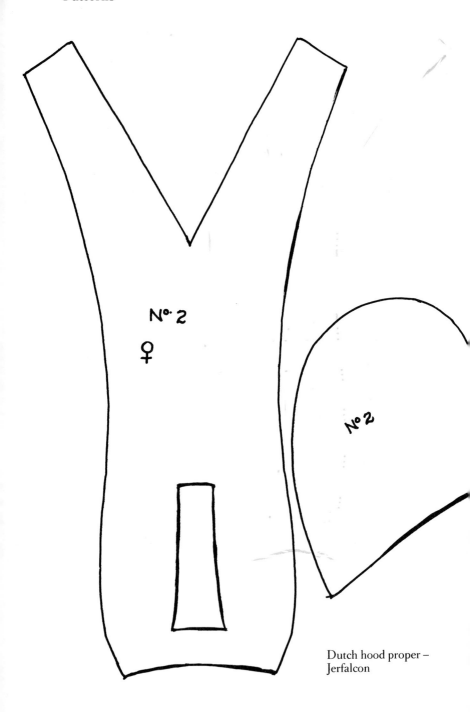

N⁰· 2

♀

N⁰ 2

Dutch hood proper –
Jerfalcon

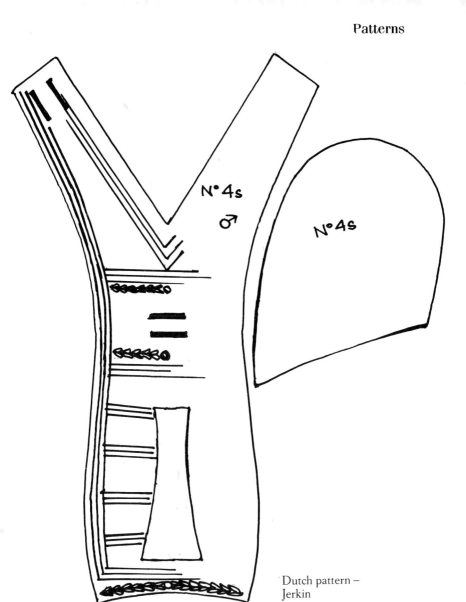

N° 4s

♂

N° 4s

Dutch pattern –
Jerkin

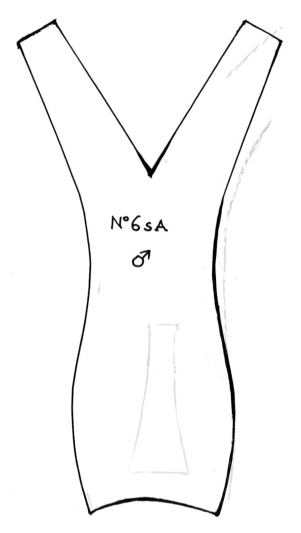

N°6sA

♂

Dutch pattern – peregrine male

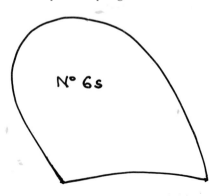

N° 6s

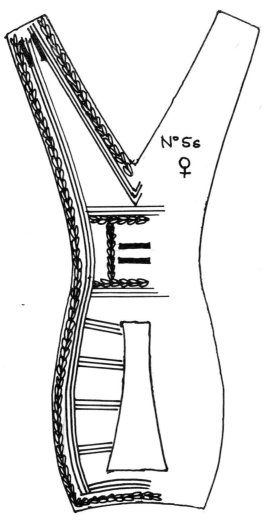

N° 5s
♀

Dutch pattern – peregrine female

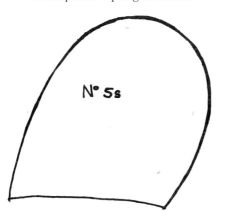

N° 5s

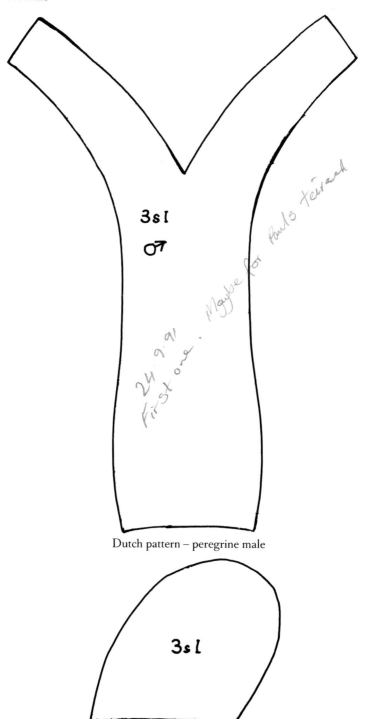

3 s l

♂

24.9.91
First one.   Maybe for Paul's teiraad

Dutch pattern – peregrine male

3 s l

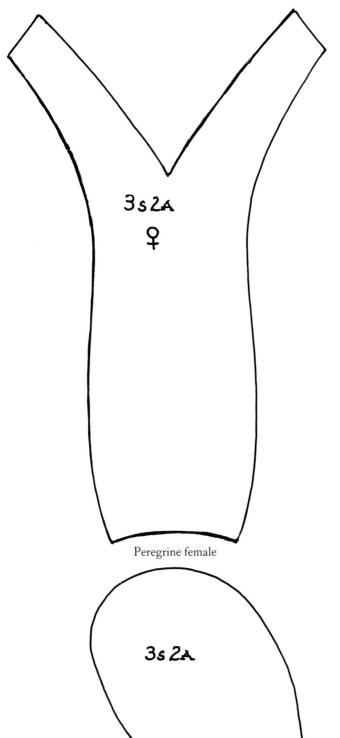

3s 2A

♀

Peregrine female

3s 2A

Patterns

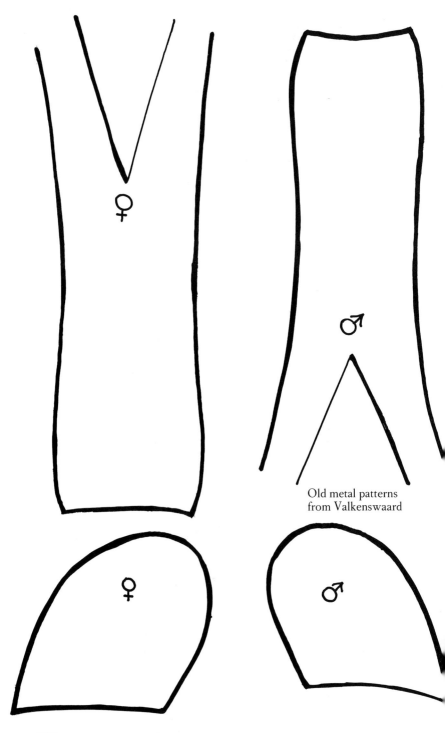

Old metal patterns
from Valkenswaard

210

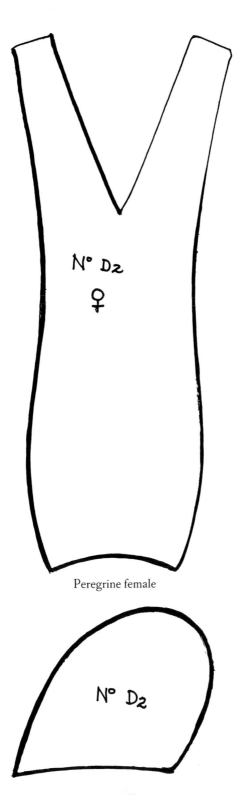

N° D2

♀

Peregrine female

N° D2

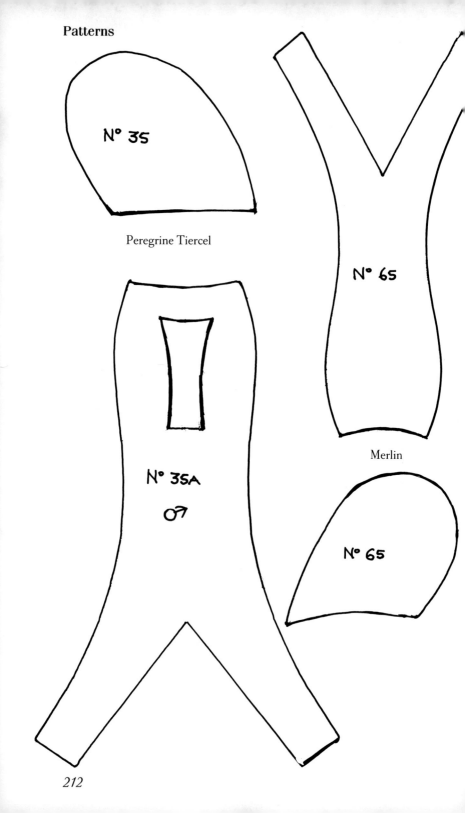

N° 35

Peregrine Tiercel

N° 35A

♂

N° 65

Merlin

N° 65

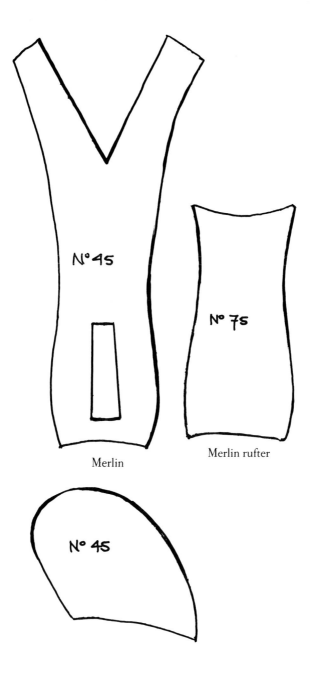

Nº 45

Nº 75

Merlin

Merlin rufter

Nº 45

Patterns

Dutch rufter hood patterns for male and female

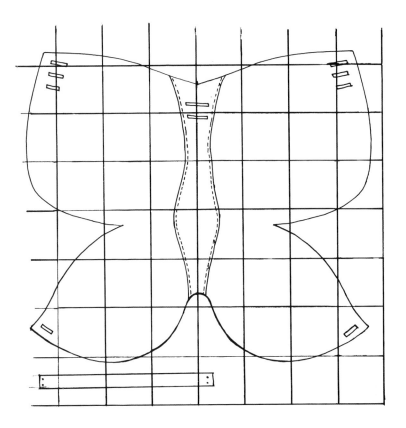

Turkistan Golden Eagle female
(enlarge squares to 1″ (2.5cm))

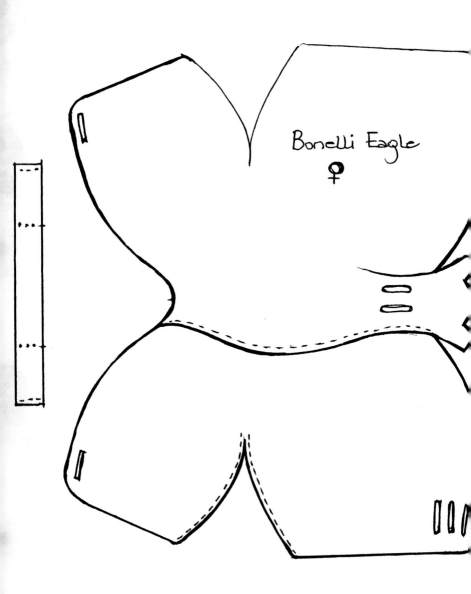

Bonelli Eagle
♀

Above and right North Afghanistan eagle hood patterns

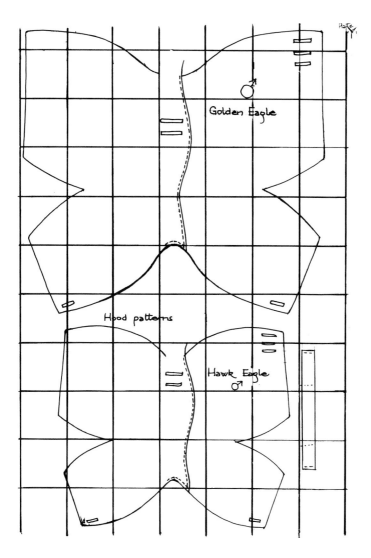

Enlarge squares to 1″ (2.5cm)

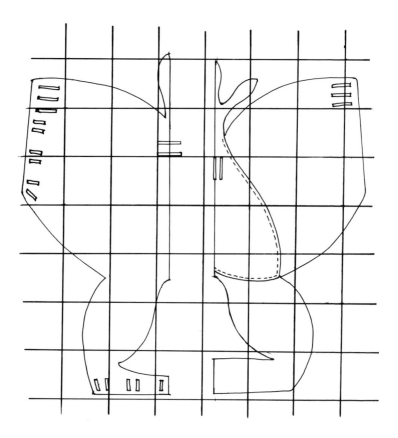

Anglo-Indian pattern – Golden Eagle.
Enlarge squares to 1″ (2.5cm)

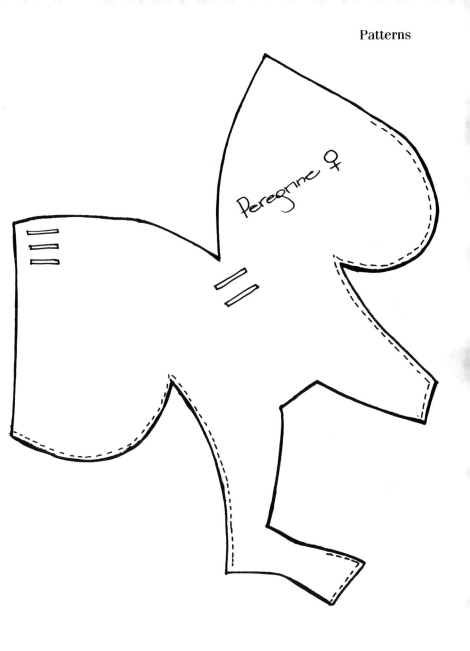

Peregrine ♀

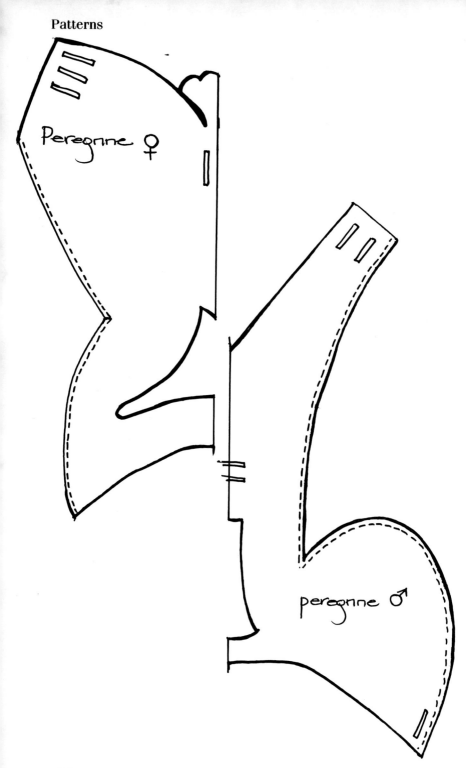

Peregrine ♀

peregrine ♂

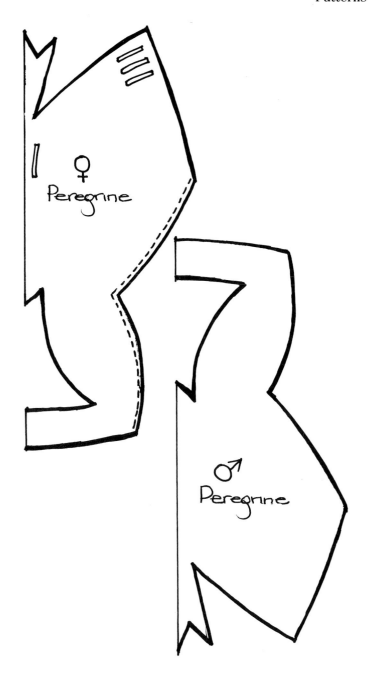

♀
Peregrine

♂
Peregrine

Patterns

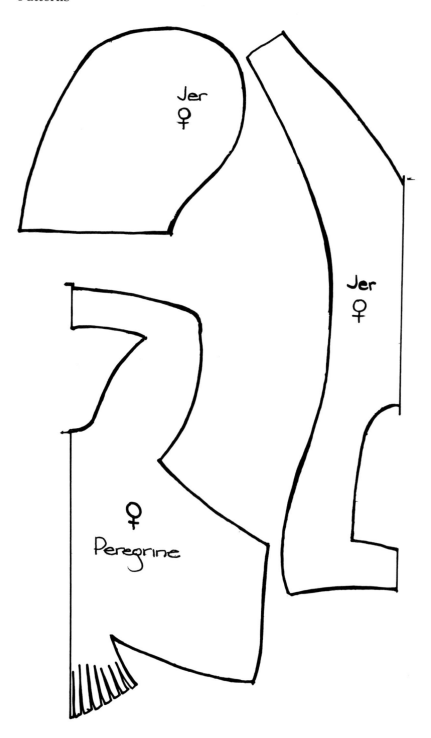

222

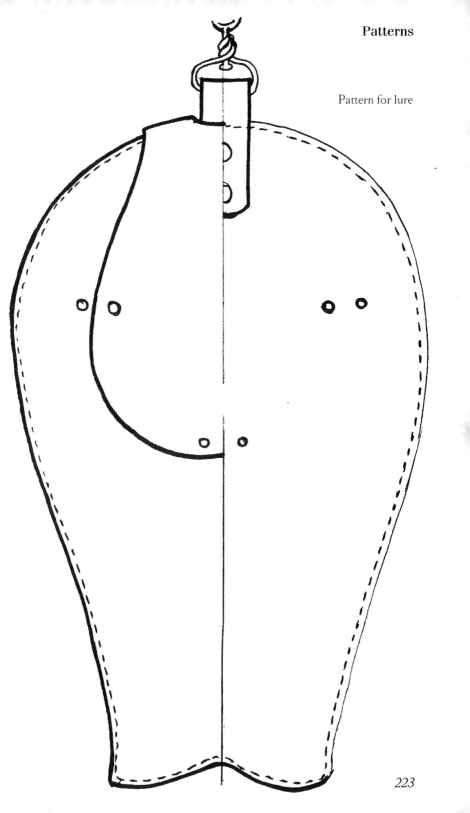

Pattern for lure

Patterns

Patterns for trimmings for hawking gloves

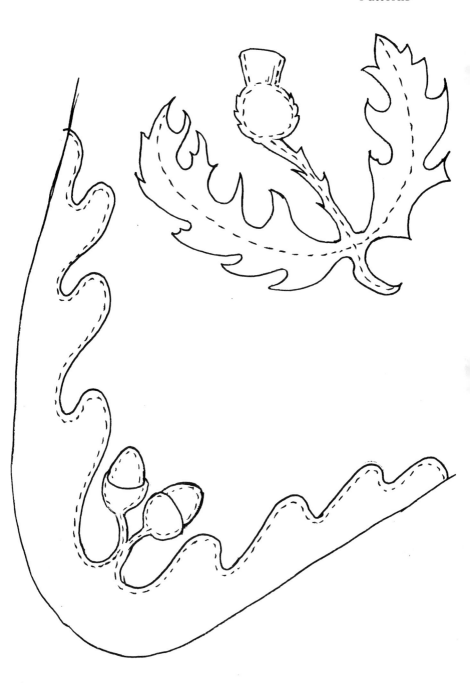

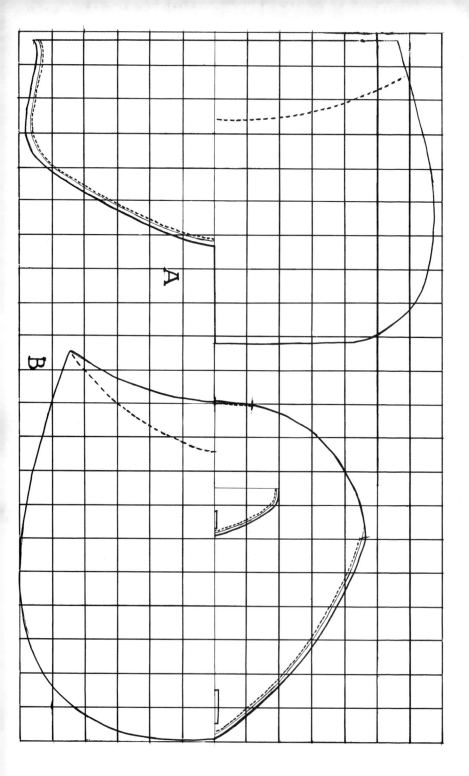

A

B

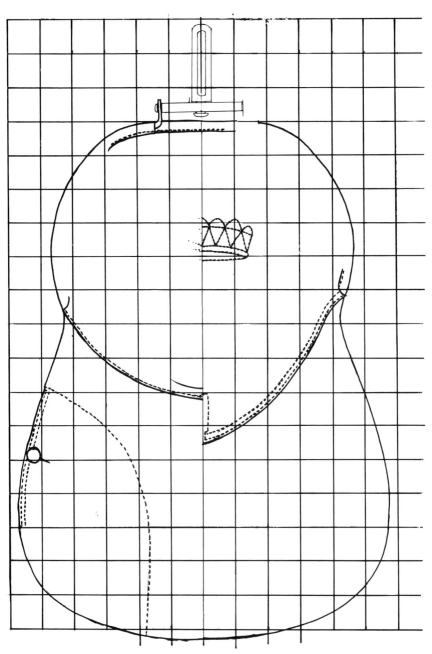

Above Patterns for Mollen-style hawking bag
Left Other hawking bag patterns (*Note* With
all these patterns, enlarge squares to 1″ (2.5cm))

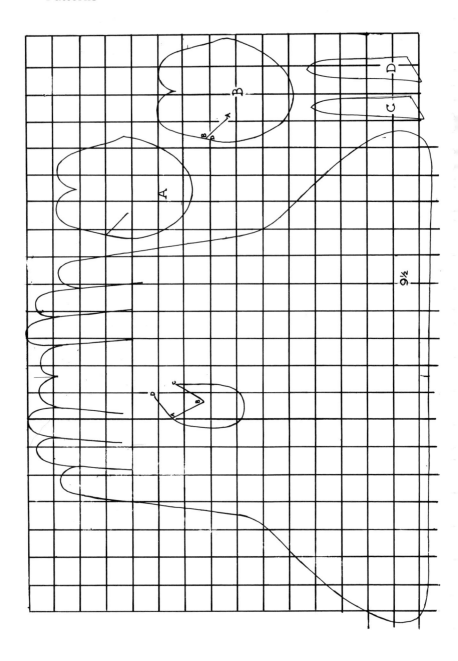

Glove patterns, size 9½. (To measure your hand for glove size use tape around the palm of the hand.) (a) Thumb pattern for single thickness glove. (b) Thumb pattern for double thickness glove. (c) Normal fourchette pattern. (d) Extra wide fourchette pattern. Enlarge squares to 1″ (2.5cm)

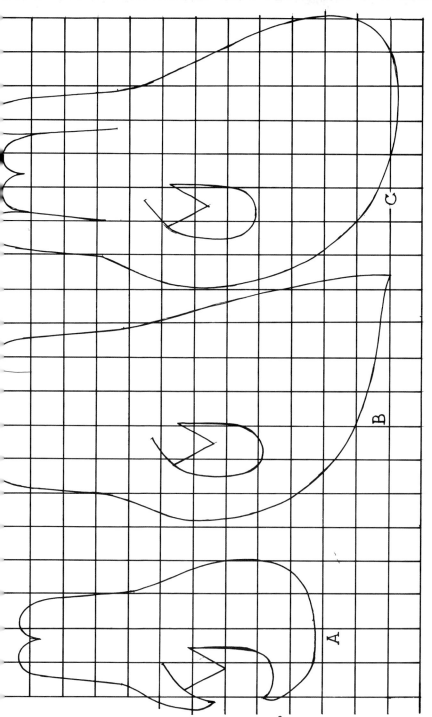

Patterns for the second layer of leather on hawking gloves. (a) To cover the wrist and the first finger only. (b and c) To cover the wrist and the first two fingers. Enlarge squares to 1" (2.5cm)

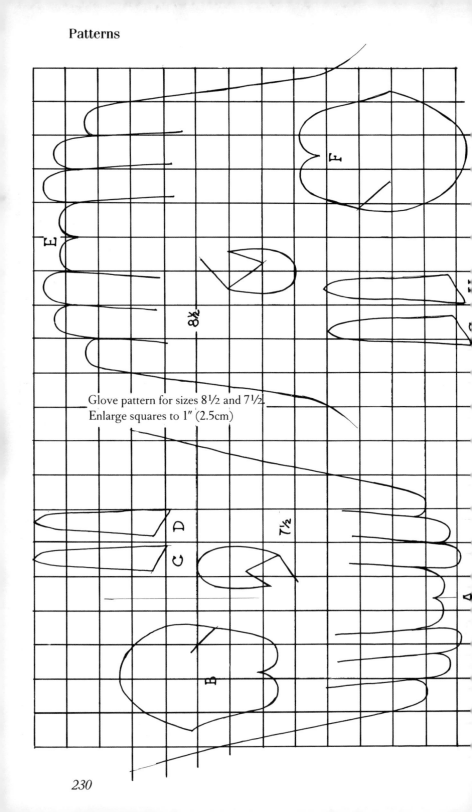

Glove pattern for sizes 8½ and 7½.
Enlarge squares to 1″ (2.5cm)

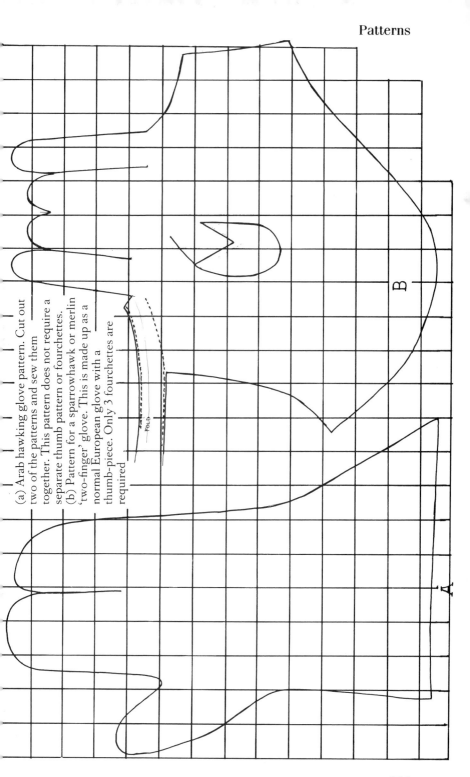

(a) Arab hawking glove pattern. Cut out two of the patterns and sew them together. This pattern does not require a separate thumb pattern or fourchettes.

(b) Pattern for a sparrowhawk or merlin 'two-finger' glove. This is made up as a normal European glove with a thumb-piece. Only 3 fourchettes are required

A

B

FOLD

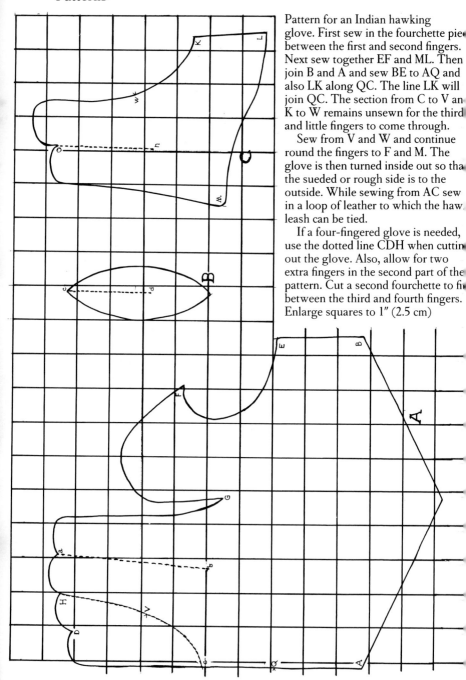

Pattern for an Indian hawking glove. First sew in the fourchette piece between the first and second fingers. Next sew together EF and ML. Then join B and A and sew BE to AQ and also LK along QC. The line LK will join QC. The section from C to V and K to W remains unsewn for the third and little fingers to come through.

Sew from V and W and continue round the fingers to F and M. The glove is then turned inside out so that the sueded or rough side is to the outside. While sewing from AC sew in a loop of leather to which the hawk leash can be tied.

If a four-fingered glove is needed, use the dotted line CDH when cutting out the glove. Also, allow for two extra fingers in the second part of the pattern. Cut a second fourchette to fit between the third and fourth fingers. Enlarge squares to 1″ (2.5 cm)

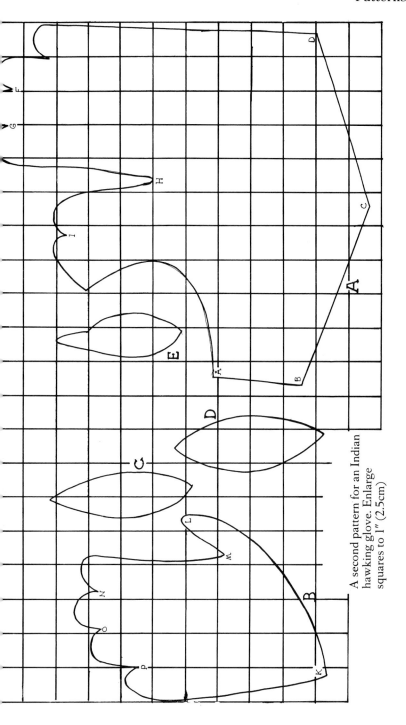

A second pattern for an Indian hawking glove. Enlarge squares to 1″ (2.5cm)

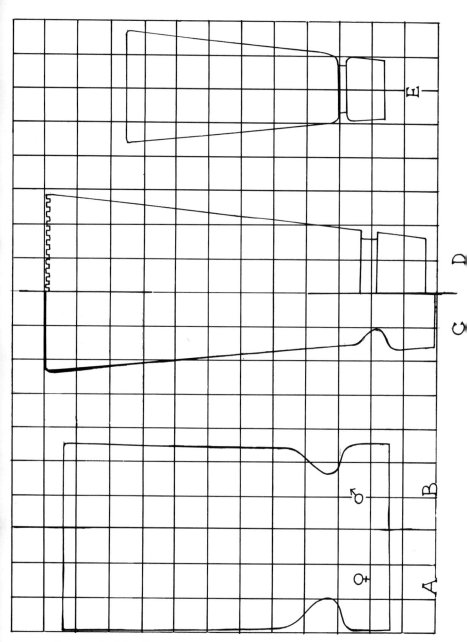

Patterns for 'block' perches. (a) Wine-glass pattern for a falcon, saker etc. (b) Wine-glass pattern for a tiercel, lanner etc. (c) Alternative wine-glass pattern. (d) Traditional pattern with groove for free-running ring. (e) Size suitable for a small falcon such as a merlin or kestrel. Enlarge squares to 1″ (2.5cm)

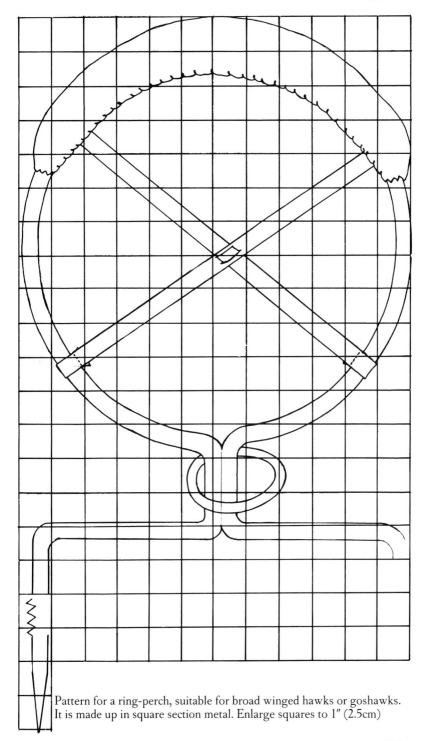

Pattern for a ring-perch, suitable for broad winged hawks or goshawks.
It is made up in square section metal. Enlarge squares to 1″ (2.5cm)

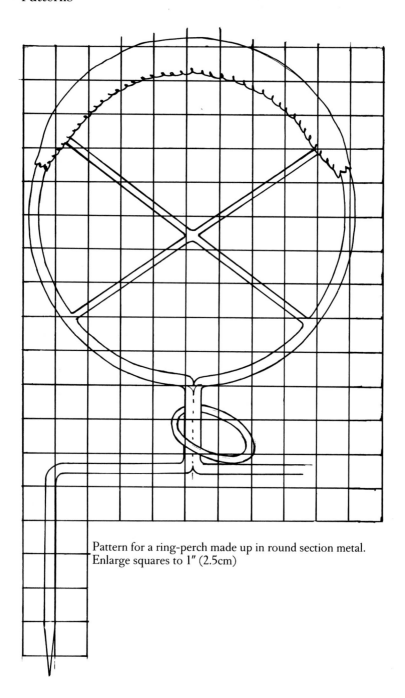

Pattern for a ring-perch made up in round section metal.
Enlarge squares to 1″ (2.5cm)

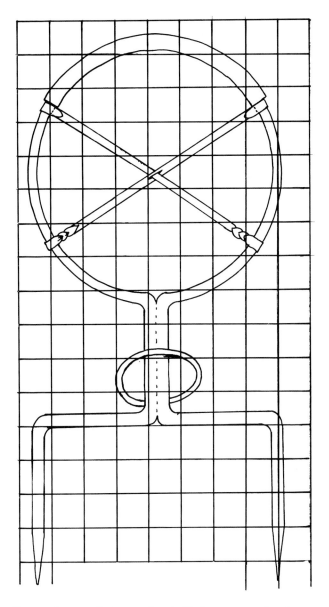

Pattern for a small ring-perch suitable for a sparrowhawk.
Enlarge squares to 1″ (2.5cm)

Suppliers

Furniture

Martin Jones (Falconry Furniture), The Lodge, Huntley Manor, Huntley, Gloucestershire GL19 3HG
Gene Johnson, PO Box 25427, Colorado Springs, Colorado 809365427, USA
Doug Pineo, 1622 Springwood Avenue N.E., Olympia, Washington State, 98506, USA
Ricardo Velarde, 1701 Newport Lane, Reno, Nevada 89506, USA
Giancarlo Pirrotta, Le Parc Verrie, 49400 Saint Hilaire, Saint Florent, France
Leathercraft of Marlborough (gloves and books), Hughenden Yard, High St., Marlborough, Wiltshire

Telemetry

Falcon Telemetrics, The Lodge, Huntley Manor, Huntley, Gloucestershire GL19 3HG
L–L Electronics, 2 Pearl Drive, Mahomet, Illinois 61853 USA
Karl Wagener, HF–Und NF-Technik-Telemetrie-An lagen, 5000 Köln 1, Herwarth Strabe 22, West Germany
Electronic Radio Falcon Distribution, Kintzheim 67600 Selestat, France
Dutch Radio Engineering, Postbus 69, 7260 AB Ruurlo, The Netherlands
Falcon Tracking System,. 459 Scarborough Beach Road, Osbourne Park 6017, Western Australia

Further reading

Allen, Mark, *Falconry in Arabia* (Orbis 1980)
Game Hawking at its Very Best: a Falconry Anthology (Windsong Press, 1988)
Glazier, P., *Falconry and Hawking* (Batsford, 1986)
Mavrogordato, J. G., *A Hawk for the Bush* (Witherby, 1960)
Mavrogordato, J. G., *A Falcon in the Field* (Knightly Vernon, 1967)
Stevens, Ronald, *Observations on Modern Falconry* (privately published in 1957)
Upton Roger, *A Bird in the Hand* (Debrett's Peerage Limited, 1980)
Upton, Roger, *O for a Falconer's Voice* (The Crowood Press, 1987)
Woodford, M. H., *A Manual of Falconry* (A & C Black, 4th edition 1987)

Index

Index

leads, dog 132
leashes 23, 26, 32–4, 38, 39, 46, 49,
    50–2, 94, 97, 98, 102, 116
leather 42
lessons 99
long winged hawks 10, 24, 32, 82
lures 22, 68, 69, 88, 102, 104–6,
    112, 120, 138, 139, 140, 172, 223
        natural 69
        preparation and care of 68–9

magpies 8, 15, 125, 126
Mavrogordato, J.G. 24, 35, 107,
    110, 116, 117, 118
merlin 8, 24, 29, 41
mews 19, 20, 22, 25
Morel, P. 40
mounting, leg 79
        tail 78

obedience 120
obtaining hawks 11
Old Hawking Club, The 19, 108,
    109, 116

partridge 7, 15, 17, 80, 133, 156–60
passage hawk 81, 93–6, 108, 120, 139
        at game 93
patterns 173–237
peregrine 11, 12, 14, 18, 19, 23, 24,
    82, 90, 107, 109, 112, 115, 120,
    122, 123
permission to hawk 8
pheasant 17, 133, 149, 157, 159, 160
pole cadge 73
positioning 144
ptarmigan 156
Pratesi, F. 90

rabbits 9, 10, 17
rain 151
responsibilities, of falconer 18
ring perch 9, 10, 17, 235, 236, 237
rings 36

rooks 8, 9, 15, 17, 80, 94, 99, 104,
    106–8, 110–13, 115–21

Saar, Prof. Dr. C. 91, 145
sakers 24, 82, 109, 110, 112, 120,
    123, 155
scales 22, 76
Shopmair, E. 73
screen perch 20, 22–4, 45, 52, 95
seagull 8, 109, 113, 122–4
serving 144
shelf perch 26
shelters 26–8
skills 10
slips 112, 116, 125
        into wind 115
snipe 160
soaring 153
sparrowhawk 8, 12, 14, 24, 38, 41,
    55, 82
sportsmanship 14
Stevens, R. 141
'sunlight and seclusion' pen 29
suppliers 238
swivels 46, 48, 94, 97, 98, 116

telemetry 15, 16, 77–80, 94, 95,
    119, 137, 138
temporary 'blocks' 39
tiercels 152
time 10
Tosti, F. 48
transport boxes 74, 75, 76
trapping 91
travel, by air 75
        by car 73
trimming 171

waiting-on 138, 142, 145, 153
weather 151
weathering 28, 29, 31, 32
weighing 76
whistles 70, 92, 117, 133
wild-taken hawks 12
woodcock 161